oe white

pure
excitement
A GODLY LOOK AT SEX, LOVE & DATING

TYNDALE

Tyndale House Publishers, Inc.
Carol Stream, Illinois

A Focus on the Family book published by
Tyndale House Publishers, Carol Stream, Illinois 60188

TYNDALE is a registered trademark of Tyndale House Publishers, Inc. Tyndale's quill logo is a trademark of Tyndale House Publishers, Inc.

Editor: Larry K. Weeden
Front cover design: Kurt Birky

Library of Congress Cataloging-in-Publication Data
White, Joe, 1948-
     Pure excitement / by Joe White.
     p.   cm
     ISBN-13: 978-1-56179-483-6
     ISBN-10: 1-56179-483-X
     1. Sexual ethics for teenagers. 2. Teenagers—Sexual behavior. 3. Teenagers—
Religious life. 4. Premarital sex—Morality and ethical aspects. 5. Sex—Religious
aspects—Christianity. I. Title
HQ35.W425 1996
306.7'0835—dc20   96-41465
                                                CIP

Printed in the United States of America
16 17 18 19 20 21 /10 09 08 07 06

Contents

Like Pieces of a Puzzle

Today as I worked through the heart of this book a letter arrived from a 16-year-old friend in Mississippi. It expressed so perfectly what I hope and pray this book will do for you:

Dear Joe,

I sat down and read your letter, and it made me feel so good to know that you care. I thought about the things you said, and I've been trying to not let it bother me if someone ridicules me. I have found a new group of friends. Two of them are Christians, I think I have been a whole lot happier, and your letter was really an encouragement to me. I have my head on straight, and I've been concentrating on the things that

matter—family, friends, grades, and, most importantly, my walk with Jesus. Thanks for your help.
Love in Him,
Morgan

Much of the collegiate and high-school mail I receive contains broken pieces from the growing-up puzzles of kids' lives. Most of the broken pieces relate to sex.

This book is simply a personal love letter from my mailbox to yours. I hope it will be a preventive letter to keep your puzzle from breaking. But if yours already has some broken pieces, my dream is that this book will be the puzzle box top, with a beautiful picture of the finished puzzle, so together we can put yours back together as perfectly as it was intended to be.

To help us turn the puzzle pieces into a masterpiece, let me introduce you to a friend of mine with a familiar name.

Adolph Coors V. The name alone buzzes your mind with a jillion wild connotations. What's the first thought that enters your imagination about him? Let me help you with a clue: He's 23 years old.

Now how do you picture him? Want another clue?

He's single . . . and a well-buffed athlete to boot.

Got a picture now?

He's 6'3" tall and as handsome as a model. He has a smile that could melt ice in a Chicago winter.

Got a better picture?

Before you get too carried away, let me paint the real portrait at the risk of bursting your bubble of expectation.

Adolph goes by the name Shane. Yes, he's a Coors; yes, he's an heir to the Coors brewery throne. But because of his dad's convictions, their branch was pulled off the family business tree when Shane was young. Shane is as rare as a pearl in an oyster shell. He's a strongly committed Christian, doesn't drink a drop of alcohol, possesses his virginity with humble security, and will soon (at the time of this writing) marry the first girl he's ever loved.

Shane Coors, Rebecca Hurst, and I work together and have spent the last two weeks running around America, recruiting staff for our summer camps. Between university visits, we discussed the upcoming wedding and all the hoopla, ceremonial details, ornamental traditions, and expectations that accompany the matrimonial extravaganza.

Yes, we also discussed the honeymoon. As we sped down the road in our truck at midnight, somewhere between Kansas City and my Ozark home, those two lovebirds and I played in our minds with the fun, the anxieties, and expectations of a Christ-centered honeymoon. Soon those two unspoiled lovers, passionately attracted yet purposefully naive, would discover God's carefully designed plan of indescribable splendor through spiritual, emotional, and physical oneness.

A romantic novel couldn't have improved the scene beside me. Rebecca sat next to Shane, with her beautiful brown eyes sparkling like diamonds, as I tried to describe the adventure that awaited them. Her dimples revealed her pleasure as she squeezed her fiancé's hand tightly.

Shane's patient demeanor gave her great security, and the Spirit of God that filled her heart enveloped her dreams with peace and harmony.

In *my* heart, I desire intently that their scenario could be yours. Perhaps I know you, or perhaps this book is our first introduction.

Perhaps you're in love; maybe you want to be. Perhaps you're 13, or maybe you're 21. Perhaps you're naive, or maybe you've been there many times. Your heart may be intact, or it may lie in many broken pieces. Perhaps your eyes sparkle with expectation, or perhaps they're stained with tears.

But let me assure you, unlike *Seventeen* magazine or *Glamour* or advice from Dr. Ruth, this book is not about hopeless regrets or illusive expectation. It's about love . . . real love . . . never-ending love—no matter who you are, what you've done (or haven't done), or how many times the misuse of sex through television, movies, or real-life experiences has left you reeling from disappointment.

Yes, Rebecca and Shane's romance would make even the hardest heart long for a similar personal encounter. And maybe theirs is a love story that seems rare in this condom-crazed, sexually distorted society we've created.

But I've seen too many thousands of similar relationships bloom before my eyes to be superficial when I say, "This love story could be for you." God didn't reserve true love only for the perfect; He reserved it for the willing. Great honeymoons don't require halos; they simply require legitimately forgiven hearts and well-instructed intentions. Yes, bodily virginity is highly preferred and biblically exhorted, but it's not required. "Spiritual virginity" is available to all true believers, and a vision of the finest that love has to offer is yours for the asking. If you want it badly enough, read on with sacrificial commitment and openness to the blueprint the Creator of the universe drew when He paused to invent "nothing but the best" in sexual oneness in the confines of lifelong marriage.

Great Sexpectations

The big, drippy tears that rested against his lower eyelids and dampened his long, brown lashes said everything about the sincerity of his heart.

"I want that picture you just painted so I can hang it in my room," the big, strapping, 15-year-old football player said.

I had just finished a heart-to-heart talk to several hundred rambunctious teenagers at our sports camp. In the course of it, I had painted a descriptive (and not very professional) picture to illustrate my message.

The subject was sex. The audience became intensely inquisitive and thoughtful as I described God's incredible plan for a lifetime of love, satisfaction, fun, and yes, sexual intimacy in His most exciting plan for a man and a woman—committed marriage.

"What's your name, and why do you want the picture?" I asked as I picked up on his moment of sensitive reflection.

"Uh, my name's Jason, and, well, you see, when I turned 15

this year, my dad gave me a condom and told me to put it in my wallet. He said I might be needing it when I was out with a girl—you know, if we wanted to have sex or something."

Wow, I thought, *what kind of crazy father would do something so bizarre?* "So," I asked, "why do you want the picture?"

"Well," he continued, "I knew he was wrong for suggesting that, but I didn't know why. Tonight you told me what he didn't. I want what you were talking about tonight. You see, I need the picture to hang in my room as a reminder, so I won't make a mistake. I don't want a one-night stand. I want my love life to last."

Guess what? Jason is 18 now, and we're close friends. He has held on to his sexual purity. He's had countless chances to take out a girl who'd spoil his vision for his marriage, *but he has a dream,* and he's determined that no sexual temptation is worth the price of "waking him up" and ending his dream. Jason called me recently, as he had become attracted to a special girl, and we had the best time discussing how he could establish a creative, fun relationship with his new flame that would eliminate sex as a pressure and a worry.

"Where there is no vision, the people perish," Proverbs 29 says (KJV). Without "great sexpectations" (that is, a personal vision for a 50-plus-year love life with your "bride of your dreams" or "Mr. Right-knight-in-shining-armor"), countless young victims will continue to succumb to the unprecedented sexual pressures applied by the oversexed media. Those media constantly promote the lie that virginity and true love are nothing more than a fleeting childhood fantasy.

They couldn't be more misleading.

They couldn't be more dead wrong.

You see, our God is a *very* creative God.

Our God is a *very* loving God.

Our God is by far the greatest inventor of all time.

Our God is also One who likes good things to be *the best,* and He desires the best things in life—like love, sex, and intimacy—to last for a lifetime. He's not interested in sponsoring a cheap substitute.

I'm a biologist by education and continue to study the science of creationism with a passion. There's no doubt in my mind that God created Adam and Eve. (The Appendix contains a summary of my personal study.) And it dawned on me not long ago that the first thing Adam and Eve probably did after they stopped gawking at each other was to discover God's gift of sexual oneness. Sounds crazy, but I'm married, too! That's the way God intended sex to be!

Take a creative, loving, pleasing God, add a man and a woman with wedding bands and two hearts united 'til death do them part, and you've got a combination that proves true love is better than you ever dreamed it would be.

I've been married 25 years, and holding my bride's hand and kissing her tenderly is still more satisfying, dearly affectionate, and fun than it was the time before. My wife is fantastic. I love her more today than I did the day I slipped the diamond ring into the surprise packet in the Cracker Jack box I handed her atop a beautiful Ozark mountain 25 years ago!

Meanwhile, the condom-crazed, neon-lighted, media-blitzed, alcohol-filled world looks for new ways to gain personal satisfaction every day. Forty- and 50-year-old men and women fill the singles' bars and erotic video rental stores like mosquitoes on a Mississippi swamp . . . searching, stalking, hiding, wishing, looking for love in all the wrong places.

As I said earlier, I receive a lot of letters from teenage

friends around the country, and my favorite part of my work with kids at our sports camp is talking through hurts and finding solutions to their problems.

I've reproduced below some of what they've told me. These are real stories with real people just like you. I pray that they'll help you solidify your thinking on this all-important area of your life.

Rob

I had been dating this girl for about five or six months. She was my first real girlfriend. After a few months, I started testing her and how far she would let me go. She kept letting me do whatever I wanted. Well, I believe we went too far. We never had sex, but it got to the point where all we would do on dates would be hug and touch each other. I knew it was wrong, so I started becoming very guilty about all that was taking place. We were best friends, and now we only talk every once in a while. It took a year before I asked God to forgive me for what I had done. During that year, I had many nightmares about what I had done to this girl and felt so guilty. I still have bad memories of the experience, and I know that the devil keeps bringing it up, but I also know God forgave me for what I did. I believe it was a learning experience I will never forget.

Jennifer

In September of this year, I had the biggest crush in the world on this gorgeous college guy. I was only

16, so I thought I had no chance with him. One day, though, one of his closest friends told me he was interested in me. I was ecstatic. Guys never noticed me before, and now I had a chance with an incredible college guy. I thought everything was perfect. When he finally asked me out, I was shaking so hard. I thought there was no way things could get better, and they didn't. Everyone warned me about him. I didn't hear one single good thing about him, yet I still liked him. My brother begged and threatened me about it, but I wouldn't stop. Our first date passed, and he didn't try to kiss me, so I thought there was no way he was using me. On our second date, we went to the movies. I was so nervous because I'd never kissed anyone before, and I thought he would try. He did, and I did kiss him, which led to light petting. After that, he wouldn't stop. I kept saying no, and he kept trying. I pushed him away, and he tried again. It scared me, but not enough to stop liking him. On our third date, everything went wrong. We were alone together, and first thing, he kissed me; then he took me over to the bed and turned out the lights. Things started getting pretty intimate, so I started pulling away. He wouldn't let me, though. I started saying, "No, no," over and over again, but it was like he didn't hear. He pinned me down and did different things to me. I just kept saying, "No." He started saying things in a mean tone like, "Don't be a baby," "Grow up," "Stop trying to be so good all the time." Things happened that night too terrible to describe.

Michael

I messed up big time my junior year of high school. I started having regular sex with my girlfriend. I was a Christian, therefore the momentary pleasure was there, but the relationship was a miserable one. I am still scared from the instances that took place. It took me until the summer before my freshman year at college (during camp) before I realized that God had already forgiven me, but I wasn't letting go. I found out that I have to totally let go of something to keep it from holding me down. I will never completely forget what happened during my junior year in high school. But I worship an awesome and forgiving God. I know I shall reap what I sow, and that is the most important thing to know. I can't tell you how ashamed I am, all because of a few months of pleasure. The biggest statement I would like to make is the fact that I would give anything to take it back and to have my virginity still to this day. Hang on to it; you will only know later how happy you'll be!

Jason

I have made many mistakes in my life, including having had sex once. Afterward, I felt very bad and empty inside. I prayed and prayed that God would forgive me for this very, very stupid mistake. I felt whole once again afterward (after praying). That is important to me, because I know that He is always there for me no matter what I do, as long as I ask for His forgiveness. To me, there is no such thing as "safe sex"; the only safe sex is when you're married.

How can God's perfect picture of our sexual intimacy, framed so carefully in His delicate plan, be that shattered and yet subsequently mended so perfectly? I believe the answer is found in the heart of the Master Painter Himself. You see, He paints the original, and He alone can repaint the portrait and remount it in a more secure frame, the cost of which is a gold wedding band.

As God visited planet Earth in the flesh for 33 precious years, He opened a picture window into His fatherly heart through the eyes, hands, ears, and voice of His Son, Jesus Christ. His view of personal failure in sexuality comes through loud and clear in the book of John, chapter 8.

The scene described there was chaotic and real to the core. The one who made you and controls your destiny was confronted by a mob of pious religious leaders dragging a half-dressed woman who had just been caught sleeping with someone else's husband. She was embarrassed, dismayed, and frightened for her life.

The law of the day stated that such a woman should be stoned to death (as well as the man involved). Yet Jesus' law was summed up in one word: *forgiveness*. The religious leaders brought the woman to the Christ to trap Him between two laws. He was definitely caught between a rock and a hard place!

"What should we do with this woman?" the religious leaders questioned with stones in hand, ready for the public killing ceremony.

As always, Jesus was adequate for the occasion. And as always, He was full of surprises. Instead of answering the question orally, He simply wrote on the sandy ground with His finger. We don't know what He wrote, but I speculate He was drawing attention away from the embarrassed woman and onto Himself. Perhaps He was writing, at the feet of some of the men, the room number at the local Holiday Inn where they, too, had entered into sin.

Whatever He wrote, it set them back on their heels. Then the knockout punch was thrown when He said, "Let the one among you who has not sinned cast the first stone."

The eyewitness account says they all dropped their stones and *split.*

Jesus then turned to face the woman with the same tender eyes with which He views you today, and He said, "Woman, where are your accusers?"

She saw that they had run away and replied, "There are none, Lord."

To which God's only Son replied, "Neither do I condemn you [You are loved; you are accepted; you are forgiven.]; go your way. From now on sin no more" (John 8:11, paraphrased).

She did as she was told. She clothed herself with the righteousness of Christ and became one of His closest followers.

Through tears of gratitude, I see Him repeating His miraculously forgiving words to teenagers when they come to me as a guide to the cross of Christ.

"Jesus Christ is the same yesterday and today, yes and forever" (Hebrews 13:8).

Diane, at age 14, has already learned how real His forgiving touch can be. Here's her story:

Diane

I slept with a guy. I'd known him for a long time but hadn't seen him in a while. When we saw each other, we both noticed each other. He was good friends with my older brother, so he'd come over a lot. Every time he came over, we would flirt and talk a lot. My family joked with me and said we liked each other, but I always denied it. One day, my family went out of town and left me at home. Someone was staying with me, but she didn't get to my house until late that night. My brother's friends (like four of them) stayed at the house to look out for me. After everyone left, that one guy came back. We kissed and "messed around," then he left. But he started calling me. Every time he came over, we would somehow end up alone. We would talk and laugh and kiss. He made a remark about how I should sneak out and come to his house. Being only 14, I thought that would be cool, so one night I did. I didn't plan on having sex with him, but one thing led to another, and I did. I told him I didn't want to, but he said, "You know you're going to do it, so would you rather do it with me or would you rather it be someone else?" I thought for a second and still said no, but when he wouldn't give up, I just went for it. I thought I'd end up doing it anyway, so I might as well do it with someone I knew real well. We still talked and were friends, and a few weeks later, I snuck out again and slept with him again. We remained friends for a few weeks, then some people found out, and we stopped talking to each other. I saw him recently when I was out with my friends; I said "Hi." He said the same, then he introduced me to his girlfriend, but not with my name. He called me "Matt's little sister." I thought, When do I get my name? When will I stop being the "little sister"? I knew then how shallow and foolish the whole thing was. I deeply regret what I did. I've made a promise to myself and God that I will never do it again. I've made my boundaries so I'll never do anything like that again. God has forgiven me, and I'm a spiritual virgin again. Although this is my second virginity, it will be with me until I'm married.

With that kind of commitment, you can look ahead with real hope. I believe your fondest dreams can become reality if, while you're reading this book, you'll ask and answer this question: In 20 years, when you're happily married, what will you wish you would have done this year?

In 20 years, if you were to look back at your "dating era" and write a personal autobiography about your intimate moments, how would you want it to read? Let the following story help you write a great one in your mind.

Ken Poure is a dear friend, an ex-used-car dealer, as funny as a sideshow, a satisfied husband, and a dedicated father. When his 16-year-old son came to him for advice one Saturday night, Ken's fatherly response gave his son wisdom that has lasted him throughout his dating and married life. The conversation went something like this:

"Uh, Dad, about this date I'm going on tonight . . . I'm a little nervous and need some advice."

"Yeah, sure, Buddy. What's bugging you?"

"Well, uh, what do I do—I mean, how do I treat her?"

"Well, Son, let me ask you a question. Do you plan to marry her tonight?"

"No. Hardly. This is just a date."

"Do you think someday your date *will* marry someone she loves?"

"Sure, I suppose so."

"Son, let me ask you another question. Do *you* plan to marry a real special girl someday?"

"You bet. Someday I'd love to do that." The lad became more thoughtful.

"Do you suppose the girl you plan to marry is out there somewhere tonight on a date with another guy?" The dad had landed his punch.

"Hmm," the boy responded carefully. "Yeah, maybe so. Maybe my future wife is on a date with someone else tonight."

"Well, Son, how do you want that boy to treat her tonight?"

"If he lays a hand on her, I'll kill him!"

"Okay, Son, if you'll just treat your date the same way you want your future wife to be treated, you'll always know exactly how to treat her."

In 1 Corinthians 6:19 and 7:3-4, God lovingly says that your body belongs to God first (who created it and bought it with His Son's own blood) and to your husband or wife second.

Why would you ever want to give the two most important people you'll ever know second best? What thinking, caring person would want to tarnish someone else's greatest gift to his or her husband or wife?

God's purposes for sex are to produce babies, to express love such as no one but happily married people will ever know, and to bring pleasure to one's mate. Plain and simple, God put the fun in sex—no fear, no guilt, no remorse, no condoms to diminish the natural intimacy. No regrets, just freedom.

The writer of Hebrews pleads with us all, "Let the marriage bed be undefiled"—that means "perfectly pure" (Hebrews 13:4).

Why do people get tired of each other? Why do they divorce? Why do so many married people continue to practice the promiscuity they indulged in before marriage and cheat on their spouses? Why, at age 25, 30, or 40, do so many adults continue to look for more satisfaction? I've read surveys through the years that suggest that as many as 60 percent of married couples cheat on each other.

It's so sad, but it's true. They missed it when they were teens, and they continue to miss God's plan.

Sexual oneness is about 10 percent physical. "What?" you say.

Yes, sex is only about 10 percent physical. The remaining 90 percent of sexual meaning, satisfaction, bonding, and pleasure is spiritual, emotional, and mental.

That's why I can't describe to you how loving Debbie-Jo is more wonderful every day and every year. I can't *imagine* going somewhere else for love. It's all so complete with her. I'm head-over-heels, out-of-my-mind in love with that girl!

Yes, lust has been a struggle for me, too, since puberty, and I've made mistakes I'm too embarrassed to put on paper. But Debbie-Jo and I made a commitment when we started dating. First, we would serve each other and put the other's needs first. Second, we would forgive each other when we made each other mad. And third, we would save sexual intimacy for our honeymoon.

Was it difficult to wait? *Yes.* Was she attractive to me? Beyond description. Did we struggle with lust? Yes.

But in waiting, we built trust. In waiting, we built respect. In waiting, we avoided guilt. In waiting for the honeymoon, we let each other know there would never be anyone else as long as we lived. Guys and girls, *that's* called freedom. Freedom in the mind, emotions, and spirit is what makes the marriage bed *all* it's supposed to be.

What about the failures you and I have had? Read on with great anticipation.

Just Like You

I'll never forget her face as long as I live. The amazement and wonder were written across it like a giant, neon billboard. Her rosy life story (like most of ours) had many beautiful petals, but some were scarred and torn. Sheila was about 16 the night she and I met one recent summer. I had addressed her and her camp friends on the subject of God's incredible love for His kids and His stellar determination to tell every teenager that *no matter what*, if they would turn to Him, they would be forgiven . . . completely . . . for everything.

The talk hit Sheila like an earthquake inside her heart. For the first time, she understood. Although her life had blemishes, in Jesus she was as perfect as the first snowflakes in December.

"Why?" she asked me, somewhat bewildered. "Why does God love me so much? Why did He die for me?"

I gently grabbed the sides of her shoulders and tenderly spoke words that flashed into my mind—words that overwhelm me to this moment.

"Sheila," I said, "He did that because He wants a little girl *just like you*."

Just like you. He wants a daughter just like you. He wants a son just like you!

If God were to carry a billfold with pictures in the little, clear strip where you pack all your best friends' school pictures, He'd carry your picture there.

Can you dig that?

If He had a bulletin board (maybe He does), your picture would be on it.

"Therefore if any man is in Christ, he is a new creature; the old things passed away; behold, new things have come" (2 Corinthians 5:17).

When Jamie, my oldest daughter, was seven and a half, her heart was firmly encamped in a rigorous gymnastics school. The training was hard, but she felt the rewards were worth it. We would travel to gymnastic meets throughout the winter and fill our lives with the cheers and tears of the competitive gymnastics world.

One evening, Jamie came home from practice. A quick glance at her face told me this evening was not like the rest. She had just been cut from the A team and placed on the B team.

As tears streamed down her face and disappointment broke her heart, I pulled her onto my lap, and we rocked in the rocking chair as only daddies and little girls can do. I began to console her by telling her the many stories of when I had been cut from an A to the B team, and worse. I looked her in the eyes, brushed away her tears, and said, "Jamie, God doesn't care what team you're on. He only cares about your heart. And little princess, you have the biggest heart of anyone I know."

After about 25 minutes, she seemed to be okay. She bounced out of my arms and was on her way back to her happy, carefree world. That night, as I tucked her into bed, we prayed together and memorized our nightly Bible verse, then I walked quietly toward the door. Just as I got to the doorway, I heard her little voice penetrate the darkness. "Daddy," she said, "thanks for tying my heart back together tonight."

I stood there in amazement. I walked over to her bed, held my face next to her soft, little-girl cheek, and whispered into her ear, "What did you say, Peanut?"

"I just said thank you for tying my heart back together tonight."

I stammered for words. "What did you mean by that, Jamie?"

She whispered softly, "Well, tonight, when I came in from gymnastics, my heart was broken, but you tied it back together again."

Can God restore spiritual virginity to someone who has had premarital sex? *Yes. Absolutely yes.* He does it every day.

Can God remove guilt and help you forgive yourself? Yes. He can and does every day. With God, forgiveness is instantaneous as we confess our sin and turn from it. Our own forgiveness of ourselves sometimes takes longer, but it grows as we make the right choices and live in purity.

Can God help you start all over again—set a standard called "sexual purity," where the honeymoon will be the next time for petting and intercourse? *Yes.* He can and does every day.

Can God erase the pictures of our mistakes in our minds? Yes, as we live in purity. He can, and He will. (It takes time, but as He takes over more and more of our hearts and minds, our memories can become our friends.)

"If we confess our sins, He is faithful and righteous to forgive us our sins and to cleanse us from all unrighteousness" (1 John 1:9).

Like countless others, Alicia learned these things the hard

way (and that's the most difficult way to learn a lesson as dear as the sex lesson). But she told me her true story so I could tell it to you.

Alicia

At the beginning of this year, I had a friend named Rick. Rick and I would talk forever. We became so close that our feelings developed into more romance than just a friendship. We started dating, and one thing led to another. I often wondered how far was too far, but I had decided I could stop whenever I wanted to.

Whenever I was at Rick's house, we would always go to his bedroom to be alone. He had such a large family that his room was the only place we could talk. Innocently, we would sit on his bed. After we started dating, it was harder to just sit there with each other. Kissing came first, and we found it harder and harder to stop there. Even after we became involved in heavy petting, I still believed I could stop before we actually did it. After a few months of this, I found that I didn't want to stop. Then one night it happened—we had sex. It was worse than I could even imagine. I felt dirty and very separated from God. I hated myself for doing some-thing I've grown up believing was so wrong. I had the guiltiest feeling I've ever had.

Rick walked me to my car and asked me what was wrong. I burst into tears. I told him that I hated it. I never wanted to do it again. Then Rick told me that he loved me, and the weirdest thing was that I couldn't tell him I loved him back. I had no feelings for him anymore. We sat in front of his house for a long time. We both cried. We knew what we did together was wrong.

I didn't see Rick for three weeks because he was out of town. During that time I prayed about it, not knowing what else to do. While we were separated, I realized what a real Christian relationship should be like, and I also realized that the relationship Rick and I had was the total opposite. I learned what was right and reassessed my morals. I asked for God's forgiveness and started my life over. I still care for Rick, but I know if we are to have a relationship, it must be based on God.

Now I know that "too far" doesn't mean only intercourse, but also the stages leading up to it. Too far is when you crave the physical more than the spiritual. Too far is when sexual thoughts take over your relationship. Too far is when you don't want to stop. It can be different for different people; it can be holding hands, kissing, or hugging. For me, kissing should be the limit. I've decided not to go any further than this until I'm married. With God's help, I can be pure from this day on.

Blueprint for Life:

What God Has to Say About It

I'm currently building a sports/music-drama summer camp for kids with my longtime friend Michael W. Smith. We've talked about it for years. Smitty's music is the kind you can listen to for a lifetime, and it keeps lifting your soul in a sweeter way every time you pop the CD into the boom box. But the man's sincere heart is even better than his music. This camp is going to be nuts! We're building huge towers for rappelling; simulated mountain climbing; mega G-force rides and ziplines; giant slides and trampolines (like into a mammoth swimming pool); beautiful, scenic buildings to live, eat, and play basketball in— I could fill this book with ideas and wacky plans!

Now we're in the fun stage. The concept is going from our minds to a drawing on the back of a napkin as we brainstorm at a restaurant somewhere, then to an architect's computer-generated blueprint, and finally to the real thing.

Once the blueprint is complete, the builders will construct each building in exactly the order specified. That way, when a storm blows in, the structure won't blow over. Or when about a hundred wild and crazy 15-year-olds climb to the 40-foot peak, it won't topple to the ground.

World-class construction guys build world-class structures. They *always* demand world-class blueprints. Their skilled hands follow the design to the sixteenth of an inch. The carpenters, masons, electricians, plumbers, and excavators huddle around the blueprint throughout the day, like a football team huddling around the quarterback. Then they break the huddle and work together like a family.

Folks, God has designed your "bod and brain" with *intense* care. He knows your sex life is the most complexly connected mental, physical, and spiritual part of your entire being—that it has incredible potential for intimacy and fulfillment (for example, my mom and dad took a 58th anniversary honeymoon just recently), but equal potential for absolute disaster (for example, homosexually transmitted AIDS and abortion). So He devotes a tremendous amount of His architectural blueprint to your success in building your sex life with splendor.

Ponder the following strong exhortations from His personal love letter to you for a few minutes. (You might return to this chapter often in the future, as storms blow in and out of your life and various sexually oriented decisions invade your life in the coming critical years.)

1. "Let marriage be held in honor among all and let the marriage bed be undefiled; for fornicators and adulterers God will judge" (Hebrews 13:4).

Notice God clearly called it "the marriage bed"—not the motel one-night stand, the fraternity formal after-party, the

"We're in love now" Saturday night, or even the engagement party. No, this is way too special for anything less than a "bonded by holy marriage for life" relationship.

I always wondered who the incredibly lucky man would be who would win the hand of Tori Tolles, the most fantastic girl who ever came to our camp. Even as a young teenager, Tori was everybody's dream girl. She sparkled from her heart right through to her eyes, her smile, and every facet of her personality. In college at UCLA, she dazzled many boys' eyes—and spun their heads when she'd take a stand for sexual honor in a liberal California classroom. This girl would be satisfied with *nothing but* the best. Her God was her Master. Her dream was pure as gold.

As you can imagine, her dating life was limited, although she could have had a million if she would have lowered her standard. But her junior year in college, she called, giggling like a little kid. "Joe, you've gotta meet Tom," she said. "He's incredible. He's 6'5" tall, a Rhodes Scholar candidate, ESPN Player of the Week, and he's a strong Christian and treats me like an angel."

Tom spent the next two years working as a counselor at our camp. He was everything she said he was.

In his UCLA fraternity, the guys all admired Tom. Many times in their rooms, the subject of sex came up. Guys would shoot off their mouths about their conquests, but Tom always kept his purity with humble honor.

"C'mon, Tom, surely you and Tori have a little sex, don't you?" they'd ask to numerous jeers.

"Not yet, guys," he'd say. "But the day will come when we'll have the best."

After two years of dating, Tom pulled off the most fantastic engagement party for Tori. He had a big, sparkling diamond ring, red roses galore, and a private horse and carriage that took her from her sorority house to a lavish dinner—all in total surprise. Tori was floored!

The next day, two of Tom's frat buddies (who were green with envy) cornered the big, strapping athlete in his room. "Well, Tom, how'd it go last night?" they asked. "Was the first time worth waiting for?"

Tom remained true to his calling. "Guys, you just don't understand," he said. "God didn't say 'until you're engaged'! He said 'until you're married.' I'm waiting for my honeymoon!"

Well, I was the lucky dog who got to perform their wedding ceremony. Tori's dad threw a *serious* West Coast party. Tom and Tori were like the kids in a toy store at Christmas. It's been three years now as I write this, and the party is still raging.

2. "Flee immorality. Every other sin that a man commits is outside the body, but the immoral man sins against his own body" (1 Corinthians 6:18).

My sophomore year in college in Dallas, Texas, I bought a Christmas present for my mom at a department store. Our SMU football team was preparing for a bowl game against Oklahoma University, and all the other SMU students had already headed home. A trip to the mall was a great way to kill some time between practice sessions. Little did I know that day that I'd be captivated by an 18-year-old girl with big, winsome eyes in the Christmas-package-wrapping department (of all places). Her name was Cindy, and she was a living doll. As she wrapped my mom's present, her personality reached across the table to my heart.

Two years later, she was standing at the altar in a white wedding gown, and we were taking the marriage vows that said we'd live together and love each other forever.

For one year during my last football season, we lived the

storybook dream. Life in college sports was glamorous. Dallas was a brightly lit city. Cindy had fun.

Then I graduated and went to work. My jobs as a football coach at Texas A&M and as a camp director were demanding. Cindy became disillusioned. I wasn't the man she thought I was. She needed more attention. I couldn't fulfill her needs.

Cindy became infatuated with a friend of mine named Larry. He was charming and attractive. I honestly never blamed her. This guy was really something. He didn't intend to steal her heart, but it happened. I was trying to keep her satisfied, but I was immature and had a lot to learn about love. I honestly don't believe adultery was ever involved. I still respect both of them to this day.

Cindy told me one March evening that she didn't love me anymore. The next day, she went home—to stay.

I *died* inside.

I cried for months. Many days, I'd go for long, lonely walks and sob for hours. My heart broke in half. My body ached from the top of my head to the bottom of my toes. We had joined our hearts and our bodies as one. When divorce tore us apart, it was like pulling apart two pieces of paper Super-Glued together; *they rip to shreds.*

Yes, I've committed lots of sins for as long as I can remember, from lying to my mom when I was five to "industrial-sized" sins of adolescence and young adulthood for which only the blood of Jesus could pay.

But this sin—this divorce sin—cut my guts out. It has taken me *years* to recover.

When God says that sexual sin is not only sin against Him but also against your body, He couldn't give a more descriptive warning. But alas, our blatant stupidity in this area continues to create the same painful scenario day after day after day.

Most of the "blood-stained" mail I receive involves another gutted victim of sexual sin. As one pregnant and abandoned 15-year-old girl said, "I feel like I had 200 knives go through me."

When God says "flee," He means "run for your lives," as my friend Josh McDowell puts it. If the movie theater gets lusty, walk out. If the "how are you" hug borders on sensuality, quickly exit. If the kiss leads your thoughts further, it's time to go home. If a lonely apartment is available, stay a million miles away. If she continues to proposition you, *break up.* When you think of this great Bible verse, just say a little phrase to yourself: "Run, baby, run."

3. "For this is the will of God, your sanctification; that is, that you abstain from sexual immorality" (1 Thessalonians 4:3).

I wandered aimlessly through the Rocky Mountain wilderness in northern Colorado late one night a few years ago. I was on an elk hunt and couldn't find our tent. It was a harrowing experience that would have made a great horror movie. The wolves howled all around me as I stumbled through the dark maze of giant spruce and pine trees. The stars were the only lights I could see. I was scared, frantic, and cold.

Fortunately, at camp as a kid, I had learned how to locate the North Star at the pinnacle of the Little Dipper. I followed that star with simplistic obedience, like the wise men who followed the Christmas star to Bethlehem's manger. After a few frightening hours, the path to the star led me to a road, and then to a farmhouse and a warm, safe bed.

Single or married—teenager, college student, or adult— the maze of sexual choices can be equally bewildering for all. The typical relationship-advice column is the biggest joke in the newspaper. But the true North Star in the sky (it's *always* hovering over the North Pole) is God's Word! When the way is beguiling, the night is dark, the wolves that want to devour your dreams are everywhere you turn, and the sky is full of alluring guides to distract you, there *is* a path that will lead you to the road to safety every time.

Look to the Bethlehem Star every night. I've simply got to have God's Word every day. That Rocky Mountain night is the way life has always been for me, spiritually speaking. Without God's clear pathway, I'd be pitifully lost forever.

As much as I've read God's love letter, I've seen only two places where He says in exactly these words, "This is God's will for you . . ." He couldn't be more directly to the point when He says, "Hey guys, you've gotta get this straight. Sexual immorality—any sex outside marriage—is a huge mistake. Don't do it." Don't do it. Whether in the mind, with the fingertips, or in direct intercourse, don't engage in sex . . . *yet!*

5

Love Is Not a Four-Letter Word

A hundred outgoing college athletes from across America and 300 high-school folks gathered up on "Main Street" of our summer sports camp. The unknown knight, in complete (head-to-toe) silver armor, proudly rode the rogue stallion into their midst to deliver the secret decree written on the scroll he carried. With sword and shield in hand, he dismounted and began to unveil his message. A few chosen friends were "in on the deal" and escorted Lori, a precious, blonde, 21-year-old staff member up to the front of the crowd.

Lori was as clueless as the rest of the gang. At camp, the out of the ordinary is the norm. Lori looked on with the naiveté that trademarked her 21 years of life. She was unspoiled by the crass world of defeated values. Lori was, indeed, a royal queen with a virgin mind, soul, and spirit.

The mysterious knight was Bo Towns, our special program director. His heart had been won by Lori over a year before this day began. But Lori didn't know when Bo would "pop the big question" and produce the precious diamond that would seal their relationship throughout their lives. The knight read through his wonderful decree in Arthurian splendor. It included a formal proposal for marriage, but it was so creatively written that it went right over Lori's head—that is, until Bo got down on his knee and opened the ring box, and the beautiful gem caught a ray of the July sunshine.

I was filming Lori's face with the video camera. Her jaw dropped half mast. She was literally dumbfounded.

The knight questioned with gallant chivalry, "Lady Lori, may I be so fortunate as to take your hand in marriage?"

She snapped into reality, almost fainted, and then melted into his arms. He lifted her gingerly onto the horse and mounted the saddle behind her. With a nudge of his boot to the horse's flank, the two romantics rode away from the crowd and out the camp gates.

Such is the expression of love at this camp we call Kanakuk. The weddings are numerous. I have performed ceremonies here for almost 25 years. None of those couples has divorced.

At a huge party one night last summer, in teams of 10, the boys gathered around a carnival booth to win the grand prize by offering the best suggestion for how to let a girl know you like her.

Guys, here's a little creative advice next time you "fall" and don't know what to say. No doubt, some of these are cheesy as anything, but give 'em a whirl anyway!

How to Let a Girl Know You Like Her:

- "If I could rearrange the alphabet, I would put U & I together."

- "Do you believe in love at first sight, or do I need to walk by again?"
- "Do you have a quarter? I told my mom I would call her when I fell in love."
- "Your father must be a thief, because he stole the stars and put them in your eyes."
- "Uh, there's this fraternity function Friday, and we've got great T-shirts for party favors."
- "I've never felt a greater pain in my heart, and I know it's love, so will you go out with me?"
- "Your knees have got to be hurtin', 'cause your fall from heaven must have hurt."
- "There ain't a camera in the world that could capture your beauty."
- Look at her shirt tag and say, "Oh, I thought you were made in heaven."
- Break ice and say, "Now that we've broken the ice . . ."
- "Do you have a map? I'm lost in your eyes!"
- Flowers in her locker
- "Made in heaven" tag
- "I forgot my number. Can I have yours?"
- "My mind is tired, because you've been running through it every day for the last week."
- "I was out last night looking at the stars, and two were missing, but I found them in your eyes!"
- T-shirt saying "I (heart) (name)"
- Her name on a sign in the sky behind an airplane
- Her name "written" in fireworks on the street
- Her name written in shoe polish on a car window
- Her name written in a gum wrapper
- "There's a movie that my mom won't let me see unless I go with someone."

- "If you were a tear in my eye, I wouldn't cry for fear of losing you."
- Her name on stadium billboards
- Block her car
- Say it in a message on your answering machine
- Pay announcer at a ball game to tell her over the P.A. system
- Call her dad and ask permission to date her
- Go up to her window and do that Romeo & Juliet thing
- "Uh . . . well . . . I was wondering . . . uh . . . well . . . maybe uh . . . we could go to . . . uh . . . the movies . . . uh . . . sometime?"
- Banner on garage door
- Beg-plead for a date
- Ring in the Cracker Jack box
- Fill her car with balloons. Have a message inside one of them. Have her pop 'em all with a pin and find the hidden invitation.

I first fell in love in the sixth grade. (It lasted at least three weeks.) Then it happened again in the seventh, twice in the ninth, and at least three other times before high school was over. None of them went anywhere, but at the time I was pretty sure I could never live without any of them.

Call it puppy love, stupidity, or whatever you please, it seems real when you feel it!

I've heard that the average person "falls in love" about seven times before he or she gets married. And there are those who say sex is okay if you're "in love." The problem with that is that your bride or bridegroom isn't supposed to be your eighth honeymoon. And to let you know how impersonal that can get, if you have sex with all seven "lovers," and each of your seven lovers has had seven lovers, then mathematically you're sharing sexual contact with at least 56 partners, because some sexually transmitted diseases, like AIDS and herpes, are not only passed on to your immediate sexual partner, but also to everyone you'll *ever* have sex with![1]

That's why my friend Wes King sings, "Don't say I love you too soon."

That's why my three buddies of dc Talk sing, "I don't want your sex until we take the [wedding] vow."

That's why God says in perhaps the most beautiful love passage in all of Scripture,

> Love is patient, love is kind, and is not jealous; love does
> not brag and is not arrogant, does not act unbecomingly;
> it does not seek its own, is not provoked, does not take
> into account a wrong suffered, does not rejoice in unright-
> eousness, but rejoices with the truth; bears all things,
> believes all things, hopes all things, endures all things.
> Love never fails; but if there are gifts of prophecy, they will
> be done away; if there are tongues, they will cease; if there
> is knowledge, it will be done away. For we know in part,
> and we prophesy in part; but when the perfect comes, the
> partial will be done away. When I was a child, I used to
> speak as a child, think as a child, reason as a child; when I
> became a man, I did away with childish things. For now
> we see in a mirror dimly, but then face to face; now I
> know in part, but then I shall know fully just as I also
> have been fully known. But now abide faith, hope, love,
> these three; but the greatest of these is love. (1 Corinthi-
> ans 13:4-13)

How Far
Is Too Far

Michelle was sweet 16 and never been kissed, although her attractive features left the boys who wanted to change that standing in a long line. She came to me one day quite bewildered because, she said, she had no hormones, could never like a boy, would never want to kiss anyone, and sex would never be an issue with her. I assured her that she was perfectly normal in every way, but that someday, the right boy would come along, and she would have a passion only God could control.

Within a matter of months, along came the school heartthrob named Nick, who not only gave her her first kiss but also wanted more—much more. Michelle discovered her affection for boys on that date, but because of her abiding faith in God and her desire for purity on her wedding night, she let Nick know in no uncertain terms that occasional kissing was her limit. Nick moved on to easier territory.

My wife, Debbie-Jo, recently remodeled her kitchen, complete with a propane-gas-powered fireplace at one end. After my great personal doubt in the planning stage, I must admit that the gas fireplace looks almost as authentic as the real thing. It's ignited by the simple flip of a switch, which sends propane gas across a pilot light that burns 24 hours a day.

With few exceptions, all of us have a "pilot light," too—a constant, small flame of passion for the opposite sex. When one burner is lit by a kiss, it's usually not long before the other burners are lit in rapid succession. Every honest person, aged 16 or 60, who has engaged in heavy kissing or petting will tell you that one burner lights the next; that heavy kissing automatically leads to desires for petting; and that if left unchecked, those desires soon become reality. "Light petting" leads to heavy petting, and heavy petting leads to intercourse.

It's good to know that God's purpose for petting is to lead a married couple into a natural, loving, gentle encounter that takes about 75 years to get over. God made petting for sex, sex for marriage, and marriage for life. The liberal philosophy of our day is, "If it feels good, do it." The problem is, breaking up doesn't feel good when petting has been a part of the program. Unwanted pregnancy doesn't feel good. Bad memories don't feel good. Guilt doesn't feel good. When a man who has had sex with numerous girls gets married and he loses his attraction for his wife (it happens every day), it doesn't feel good.

Without a doubt, a great kiss with someone you're crazy about feels good. It's supposed to! Petting feels good. But feelings don't make something right! God made feelings. He knows your feelings last forever, and He wants your emotions and your passion for sex to feel good for *life,* not to be ruined at a high-school prom.

Next time you go for a drive (if your car doesn't have manual shift), notice how the automatic transmission shifts from one gear to the next. Step on the gas and it sails smoothly from low gear to second, from second to drive, and from drive to overdrive in a matter of seconds. *That's* what petting does with sex. It's an automatic transmission to intercourse. In a picture, it looks a lot like this thermometer.

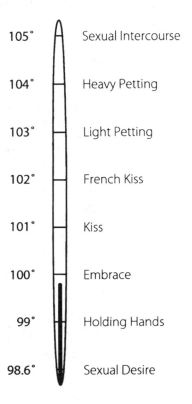

105°	Sexual Intercourse
104°	Heavy Petting
103°	Light Petting
102°	French Kiss
101°	Kiss
100°	Embrace
99°	Holding Hands
98.6°	Sexual Desire

The minute lustful desires hit and you want to go further, it becomes sin. Love waits. Lust wants. Love can't wait to give what is true and honorable. Lust can't wait to take. Love mends. Lust hurts. Love is secure. Lust is selfish. Lust ends. Love lasts.

These teenagers who have gotten in touch with me have learned the lesson the hard way:

Paul

I went a little too far with one of my girlfriends, and we ended up in bed. We really destroyed our relationship. We both regret what we did that one night. It has ruined both of our purity, and I'm sure we'll both regret it for many years to come.

Barbara

I have not gone all the way, but pretty far! This past year, I've had a serious boyfriend. We kissed for about one month, then started getting more serious. We had done other stuff, kissing and petting, but never really made out. But then we did! I still don't know what love means. We broke up about a month ago. And when I think about what we did, it makes me sad.

In a similar way, the question of right or wrong in terms of masturbation can be understood with wisdom and discernment. Masturbation is a personal sexual release that almost all boys and some girls experiment with during their growing-up days. It can be a release for a boy when his hormones get "too hot to handle." It's like the pop-off valve on the water heater.

When a water heater malfunctions, instead of exploding, a valve at the top opens and releases pressure from the tank to keep it from blowing up. It's definitely a mess and a last-resort measure—not the way it was intended to function, but better than a major explosion.

The issue of right and wrong with masturbation is the issue of lust. The sin is what goes on in the mind. If a boy looks at pornographic magazines, movies, or television, his mind begins to imagine being with the women he has seen. *That's* the sin. As God says, "Flee from youthful lusts" (2 Timothy

2:22). If a girl fantasizes over a guy and begins to have sexual desires that are reserved only for her "Prince Charming for Life," the fantasy is when the sin begins, and that's the place where it needs to end.

A sincere boy came to me for counsel one summer day at our sports camp. Masturbation had become a problem. But the thing that bothered him the most was that every time he looked at a girl, his mind took her clothes off. It was killing him inside! "What do I do?" he pleaded.

Coincidentally, my straightforward 12-year-old daughter came walking by. I asked her to sit down and, leaving out the details, asked her to advise him. She simply looked him in the eyes and said, "Mike, tell me, what kind of movies do you watch?"

He knew what his problem was immediately. Satan had won his mind, and the only thing the boy knew to do was to masturbate and mentally rape girls.

With prayer and some serious changes in his Friday- and Saturday-night entertainment, Mike won his mind back and now enjoys freedom from lust most of the time.

I can't imagine how many fewer tear-stained pillows and shattered hearts there would be if every couple at a fraternity party, high-school prom, and "first date to the movies" knew that lust was a chain reaction. If the reaction is not Christ-controlled, it begins in the mind and rushes through each stage of kissing and petting until intercourse results or the process is abruptly stopped by a slap in the face or a courageous "No!" in a steamy car on a lonely road. The result is always two frustrated people driving away, usually in search of a different date the next time around.

Petting leads to intercourse, plain and simple. When you're married, over the years of discovery together, you'll learn the process and become an expert with the one you'll love for a lifetime. But until your hearts are bonded and the ring is securely placed on your left hand, don't play with fire or the forest will soon be ablaze, and your own home will be caught in the flames.

Don't you think this is what God's Word, spoken through the apostle Paul, means when it says, "It is good for a man not to touch a woman" (1 Corinthians 7:1)? In Scripture, God applauds a man who touches the right woman in the right way at the right time, but He severely warns the man who touches the wrong woman in the wrong way at the wrong time.

A sincere Texas teenager sought advice from me one November evening as she worried her way through her first physical relationship. She had determined that "making love" (an oxymoron in itself) was too far, but she was trying to determine just how much petting was appropriate to spice up this relationship and please her boyfriend enough to keep him around. I realize that advice is about as cheap as the price you pay for it and is usually remembered about as long as it takes to give it, so I just asked her a question (and I ask the same question to you).

"Janice," I said, "tell me, how fantastic do you want your honeymoon to be?"

She quickly replied, "Nothing but the best."

I followed with the obvious question, "How much of yourself do you want to present to your bridegroom as a wedding gift that night?"

Again her reply was certain. "All of me. I want the gift to be perfect."

"Well," I concluded, "how much of your husband's wedding gift are you going to give away to the guy you're dating now?"

She quickly made up her mind that for her, the answer was "Zero."

Wedding gifts are wrapped in innocence and white lace. For guys, the gift is wrapped in a tuxedo of trust, a pure, clear mind, and patience that will wait a lifetime.

Please understand that as you decide how far is too far for you, the stakes are high—very high. And God's Word is clear—very clear.

There are those (I know them well) who are *still* on their honeymoon even though they've been married for 10, 20, or 30 years and more. Almost every night that they engage in sexual oneness, they experience a new discovery sweeter than the time before. But many, many are the couples (please hear me, I know *them* well, too) who, after only a few months or years of marriage, are frustrated, confused, no longer attracted to each other, separated, or even divorced.

Each year you wait and each phase of intimacy that you save for your spouse is a bank account of pleasure that will pay dividends "till death do you part."

It's Your Call

The most important question you'll ever answer is "Where do you want to spend your eternity?"

Second only to that question, I believe (because of the myriad ramifications that surround it), is "How do you want to manage your sex life in your teenage years and the decades that follow?"

Let me invite you to answer the following questions personally and privately:

Do you want just a wedding or a happy, lasting marriage?

Do you want another night in bed or a fulfilling, exciting honeymoon?

Do you want just a bridegroom, or do you want a husband?

Do you want just a bride, or do you want a wife?

Do you want a few evenings with occasional sexual thrills, or do you want a lifetime of sexual fulfillment?

Do you want grief and shame, or do you want freedom?

Do you want sex, or do you want true intimacy?

Do you want something that feels good, or do you want the best?

Teens who are honest with themselves, almost without exception, want the latter answer to each question. I surveyed 1,200 teenagers and college students at our sports camps in 1995, and 87 percent believe that sex is acceptable only in the boundaries of marriage. Who in his right mind doesn't want the best?

You can't have both extramarital sex and God's best. God is no fool. He reserves true love and sex in a position of highest status, accessible only to the moral, monogamous husband and wife in a Spirit-filled marriage bed.

I've seen more failures in this area, suffered by kids who've tried to circumvent God's plan, than the pages of this book could contain. Here's just one of the many letters I've received from teens who tried it out and ended up wishing they'd never heard of that three-letter word:

Robin

When I met Bobby, I trusted him to know how far we could go without making love. He was in the driver's seat. He was also insecure. He would tell me over and over how he loved me, how he was sure that I didn't love him as much as he loved me. It was then that I set out to prove it. I was his—110% his.

The first time we made love, I had no idea what was going on. Afterward, he didn't speak; he passed out. I was so alone. I've never hated myself more. But it was done; my virginity was gone. It didn't matter after that; sex became an everyday occurrence. My only fear was losing Bobby. He was the first, and even if he treated me bad (and there were those times), I was going to do anything I could to hang on to him.

Slowly we drifted apart. He wanted to go out with other girls. I loved him, and he fooled me into thinking he loved me too. The day I left for the summer, we made love—yeah, it was fun—but it was just actions. That same evening, he told me he was going to see other people.

I went through misery the next 10 days, being away and knowing I was carrying Bobby's child. I wasn't real sure, but I knew something was up. How was I going to explain this to Bobby? Then I began to scheme. I got excited and thought, "Sure, he'll want to get married." Finally I had him, and if not him, I had a part of him anyway. I wouldn't have an abortion—that was out of the question. I'd either marry Bobby or run off and have the child myself.

Funny how Bobby controlled my mind. I told him one night after we had made love down in his basement. I thought since he was so in love with me, that now was the time to break the news. He really lost it—he got all defensive and said that there was no possible way he could marry me and that he didn't even want to. I got scared and told him I was just kidding. He breathed a sigh of relief but remained cold.

It was not too long after that I told him the truth and had the pregnancy confirmed by a doctor. Bobby had stuck by his guns about not marrying me and said if I kept the child, we were through. At that point, I was helpless. I wanted more than anything to talk to my mom, but I could not hurt her with this kind of news.

Looking back now, I should have talked to her.

Bobby stuck by me long enough to make sure I had the operation. He called me every day or wrote and made me feel like he still cared. I went in that day by myself to do the one thing I was most against. I talked to Bobby that night, and then he took off. He stuck around long enough to make sure I got rid of the evidence, then left me on my own.

I can't explain the feelings I have inside me now. I've never thought less of myself or felt more like trash. How could I have been so naïve? I loved him, but he never knew the meaning of the word. I still have nightmares, and at times I hate myself. Abortion is much, much deeper than the scraping of that uterus lining. It involves the destruction of one's whole being, the loss of any self-respect, and, saddest of all, a guilt-ridden existence.

Thankfully, I've also seen many godly partners like my mom and dad, who've been married more than 50 *years* and still enjoy sexual harmony that would make Hollywood blush.

Each of them is the only sexual partner the other has ever known.

So, how do you wait for the best?

The purpose of the next few chapters will be to establish in your mind and in your lifestyle the sexual man or woman you want to be. To prove the value of what they will say, note an extensive survey done in various high schools in the state of Utah. Among the teens who associated themselves with positive (abstinence-minded) peers, had high values, and never drank, only 4.6 percent gave up their virginity in the next year. Among the teens surveyed who had negative peers and low values and who drank alcohol, 48.7 percent made the giant step from virgins to nonvirgins.[1] Drinking, peer pressure, and lack of solid values increased the likelihood of sexual experimentation leading to sexual regret by more than 10 *times*.

That's enough to make you stop and think, isn't it? Want some help? Read on.

To Drink or
Not to Drink

Dear Joe,
   Well, I've got myself in a real mess
now. See, it all happened about 2
weeks ago when I went over to my best
friend's apartment as usual to see how
she was doing. (Her name is Shelly,
and she's 19 years old and lives alone.)
Well, when I got there, she asked me if
I wanted something to drink, so I said
sure. Well, she brought a bottle of
wine, wine coolers, and beer out. I
asked her where she got them, and she
told me she has an older friend who
can buy the stuff. I had never drunk in
my life, and she knew I never did and
never wanted to either.
   Well, I don't know how it started

or why I did, but I started drinking a glass of wine. I said, "It tastes good," then I said, "A couple won't hurt me." Then the next thing I knew, the bottle of wine was gone, and so were the wine coolers (one four-pack). Then the next thing I knew, I started on a can of beer, and that night I was as alone as a bum on the street.

Joe, I'm real scared now because for one, I drank and got drunk, and for two, I did stuff that night I can't even say. And ever since that night, I've drunk six nights out of the 14 days since I started, and I haven't yet got drunk again, but I want help. Will you please help me? I've been a Christian for a very long time, and I don't want to lose to the devil.

Dear Joe,
    I care so much about people and what they do with their lives. I think it is such a tragedy to see so many teenagers today throw their lives away with drugs and alcohol. Just three days ago, two of my good friends were pretty badly injured in a drunk-driving accident. They got in the car with two guys who had been drinking, and they went into a guard rail on a bridge and went off. Needless to say, both of

my friends were also drinking. The two guys weren't hurt, and my two friends got off easy with a broken jaw, rib, and some stitches.

For years, high-school and college students have told me that drinking and sexual morals go together like Siamese twins. When you start drinking, your morals slide. Far too often, the two walk hand in hand all the way to the abortion clinic or the tear-stained pillow.

High-school students who don't drink are *six times less likely* to lose their precious virginity wedding gift than those who've drunk alcohol recently.[1]

Date rape (the ultimate oxymoron) on college campuses has risen by tragic landslide proportions in the last 10 years. Almost *all* those crimes are alcohol-related.[2] As one dean of students reports, "I don't know of one case of sexual assault where students haven't been drinking. I tell students on my campus, 'Get drunk and you run the risk of being raped.'"[3]

Thud!

Our sports camps have a staff of 1,700 collegiate Christian athletes. They're about the happiest, most attractive, fun, enthusiastic bunch of kid-loving people you ever laid eyes on. Though some have fallen during their teen years, all are committed to waiting for marriage for sexual intimacy. And get this: All 1,700 don't drink the entire time they're under our employment. Most *never* drink and won't throughout their lives.

Why? Because they don't want to cause a younger person to stumble. Because American alcohol is all considered "strong drink" and is forbidden in Scripture. And because they value their moral character.

Alcohol abuse is rampant in our country! In a recent survey

of 68,000 fourth-through-sixth-graders, perceived alcohol use has risen to 45 percent![4]

High-school kids around the country tell me that about three-fourths of the students they know drink. In college, it's more like four-fifths.

The true stories pour into my mailbox. The alcohol and drug stories all say the same thing: "Drinking and drugs rape your morals."

Sybil

One night, I decided to hang out with a good guy friend at his apartment. He was a freshman in college—I was a junior in high school. Going into the evening, I had no idea what was in store for me. I began the evening with a couple of drinks and a few shots. Very soon after that, the alcohol had overcome some of my mind. Chris, my friend, and a few of his friends were smoking pot—something I had quit and promised myself I wouldn't do anymore. I gave in to the peer pressure and soon was very high. The friends left, and Chris and I started kissing. One thing led to another, and before I knew it, I was losing my virginity. Chris ignored my "No, I'm not ready for this." Immediately I passed out. I woke up to Chris forcing himself into me very strongly. To this day, I still don't know whether I am a virgin or not. The pain, regret, and hurt I have suffered could have all been prevented if only I had thought before I acted.

Adrianne

When I drink, I do very stupid things. You aren't thinking the alcohol is controlling you, but it is. One time I got drunk at a party and fooled around with two guys. The only thing I know about them is their names. I got a very bad reputation. I got called a slut, and no one respected me. I also put my life in danger. I let someone who was high drive me home. I did all this just to be cool.

Kathy

I never thought I would regret sex so much. One night I was at a party, and I got drunk and had sex with someone else while going out with my boyfriend. I felt awful, and I was scared of diseases. Then I made myself stop drinking because I knew if I wasn't drunk, I wouldn't have had sex (not that that's a good excuse). I didn't drink for a couple of months and felt a little better.

Then I was introduced to drugs. I promise this ties in with sex. When you start smoking pot, you begin to not care about anything else. I started seeing a guy friend who sold it, and he wanted to have sex. I promised myself I wouldn't. Anyway, I did have sex with the bad guy, and I became miserable—I'm still miserable. I've hurt everything about me. I can't even be happy unless I'm faking it, which is constant.

I guess my main point is, once you have sex, even if you do love the person, it only leads to more, and eventually you'll want to experiment even more. All it is, is heartache.

Many scoffers will read those warnings about alcohol and counter, "Didn't Jesus turn water into wine?" The answer is yes, but no.

Here's what the Bible says about alcohol:

"Wine is a mocker, strong drink a brawler, and whoever is intoxicated by it is not wise" (Proverbs 20:1).

"Woe to those who rise early in the morning that they may pursue strong drink; who stay up late in the evening that wine may inflame them!" (Isaiah 5:11).

You can see that the Bible specifically condemns not only getting high or drunk, but also partaking of "strong drink." In biblical times, "strong drink" (*sikera* in the original Greek of the New Testament) referred to any unmixed or undiluted wine. When Jesus turned water into wine in John 2, He didn't make *sikera;* He made *oinos,* weak wine diluted with water. When Paul told Timothy, in 1 Timothy 5:23, that he should drink wine, he told him to do it for medicinal purposes (for a stomach problem). Again, it was *oinos,* not *sikera.* (Today we have sophisticated medicines for such needs.) According to researcher Robert Stein, in biblical times, people used wine to purify unsafe water, not as a way to get high.[5] Strong drink in biblical times was from 3 percent to 11 percent alcohol. The least ratio of water-to-wine mixture was 3 parts water to 1 part wine. That produced a subalcoholic drink that was a maximum of 2.5 percent to 2.75 percent alcohol. Normally, the ratio was even higher, up to 20 to 1. *That's 20 parts water to 1 part alcohol, for an alcohol content of less than 1 percent.*[6]

By contrast, modern American beer usually has an alcoholic content of 5 percent. Modern wines have 9 percent to 11 percent alcohol; one brand has 20 percent alcohol. Brandy contains 15 percent to 20 percent alcohol; hard liquor has 40 percent to 50 percent alcohol. According to biblical standards, these beverages would all be considered strong drink.

At age 16, Sara would strongly urge you to avoid alcohol like the plague. Like the vast majority of high-school and college students today, she had a family who didn't.

Sara, her mom, her dad, and her brother lived in the suburbs of a large city. From the outside looking in, you'd say they had it all—money, cars, action, sports, beauty (man, Sara is beautiful). All the trappings were there. But a guest named Jack Daniels always hid himself in their home, inside a bottle. You see, Sara's dad was an alcoholic. He just couldn't kick the habit that he'd begun so many years before.

During Sara's sophomore year in high school, Sara's dad died. His body just couldn't take any more alcohol. If he would have known his ill-timed fate, you can bet your last penny that he'd never have taken his first sip. But like all the others who take "just one drink" or say "Aw, it's just one or two beers," he said, "It will never happen to me."

One week after her dad died, Sara's brother was in a friend's red-hot car coming home late one night from a party. The friend was drinking, and his senses were dulled. The car left the highway and ran head-on into a tree. Suddenly, the "ideal little family" of four caring loved ones had been transformed into a lonely mom and a bewildered teenager clinging to each other and the Kleenex box, searching for answers and wondering how alcohol could be so heartless.

Nobody wants to be an alcoholic, but those beer commercials during the halftime of the Super Bowl look so innocent and inviting.

Nobody wants to be a drug addict, hopelessly trembling, begging, or robbing for the next fix. But that guy with the bag of weed who sits next to you in algebra class sure does describe that first high in alluring terms.

You see, all sin is just like that. Satan is smart. He makes the next step look so good that he blinds you from the end result.

"You know when to stop," he whispers into your ear.

"Just this once."

"One beer won't hurt anybody."

"You can handle it."

"Real men do it, so why don't you?"

The intelligent man, the woman of vision, the 19-year-old who knows what kind of parent he/she wants to be says, "*Never.*"

Here's how a friend of mine said, "Never again."

Joe,

Thanks for your letter and the book. It is very good and has helped me greatly with some problems I have been facing lately. I can feel myself changing greatly every day since I decided to let God run my life. It is truly amazing. I get so excited about life now, it is just unbelievable. Before I accepted Jesus Christ into my heart, I had a problem with drinking (and other things). My dad is an alcoholic, and my brother also is. Therefore, I believed my course of life would follow the same path. I thought there was no way around it. I began to feel really bored with life, and I found myself really dependent on alcohol. At first, I thought drinking was all right since I grew up around it. I felt it was just part of life—a necessary part of life. How terribly wrong I was! I tried to stop drinking after realizing I was putting myself in bodily harm. I told myself I was not going to drink for a month. The first night of that month was one of the toughest struggles I've been through. I felt that I needed to drink more than anything else. But I didn't. The second night of that month, I gave in. My strength was not strong enough to overcome my dependency. I felt like a failure. I knew I could not do it alone. Now, as a true Christian, I've tried to stop again. This time it was different! I asked Jesus to help me with my problem and to show me the way to a happy life, and that is exactly what He did. When I tried to stop drinking for the second time, it was one of the easiest things I have ever done. I felt no need whatsoever to have alcohol in my system. It was amazing how much easier it was that second time. But we both know why it was so easy. It was because Jesus was in the driver's seat. I no longer dislike this earth. The new friends, wonderful times, and all the better ways I look at life are just incredible. I have never been so happy, and this happiness will be growing more and more every day! I know there will be trials, but I also know that whatever comes my way, with the Lord's help, I will be able to handle anything!

9

What's on Your Mind

Are you ready for some fun, with a little amazement and mental challenge attached? Try the following memory gymnastics test, and see how you fare. To play the game, as I mention an advertising phrase, try to identify the product that used the slogan. Some of these are several years old, so you may have to dig in your memory bank to score a perfect 20.

1. "Make a run for the border."
2. "It's the real thing."
3. "Uh huh!"
4. "We run the tightest ship in the shipping business."
5. "Just what the doctor ordered."
6. "Shout it out!"
7. "You're in good hands."
8. "Have it your way."
9. "Where's the beef?"
10. "You can hear a pin drop."
11. "Like a rock."

12. "The choice of a new generation."
13. "It takes two hands to handle a Whopper."
14. "You'll love the stuff we're made of."
15. "Get a piece of the rock."
16. "Two all-beef patties, special sauce, lettuce, cheese, pickles, onions on a sesame seed bun."
17. "The king of beers."
18. "The silver bullet."
19. "Tastes great—less filling."
20. "Head for the mountains."

Okay, how many did you get? If you're anywhere close to 20, your brain is amazing, and you've probably checked in on the TV set a few times as you've been growing up.

Guess what?

Some of those slogans are more than 10 years old, and you still remember them.

You want to know something more amazing? Even though you didn't intend to remember them and associate them with the products, your mind sucked them up the way you guzzle a cold Pepsi on a hot day, and you'll never, ever forget them.

Ask your parents or grandparents what "L.S.M.F.T." means. They heard the slogan on the radio in 1958, yet more than 90 percent of those who heard it can still remember it.

Your mind is the most fantastic thing *ever* built on planet Earth.

The multibillion-dollar space shuttle can't touch your mind in its ability to create and process thoughts. Here are a few hard facts about the mind that almost all psychologists have always agreed on:

1. All your actions, decisions, and attitudes begin in your mind.

2. Your mind is susceptible to manipulation by almost any attractive outside source.

3. The 10 billion cells of your brain are like tiny rooms that capture (whether you want them to or not) every sight and sound (especially when connected with music) you'll ever see and hear.

4. Your subconscious mind absorbs thoughts even when your conscious mind doesn't ask it to.

5. And finally, you become what you think about. Or as Proverbs says, "For as he thinks within himself, so he is" (Proverbs 23:7).

The advertising departments for McDonald's, Budweiser, and all the other consumer-goods companies spend billions of dollars every year, trying to get their slogans in your head, knowing that once they are there, they will strongly influence you to buy their products. An ad during the Super Bowl costs a company more than $2 million a minute! You might be watching a football game on ESPN, but when it's over, you have this strange urge for Domino's Pizza! Oooh, those marketing guys are cagey!

Just ask Andy Hilfiger, who owns the clothing company Tommy Hilfiger. Hilfiger has enlisted musicians to promote his clothing line at their concerts. Why? Because the stars' merely wearing a certain brand has been shown to have an enormous impact on sales. On an MTV news program, Hilfiger explained what happened: "Snoop [Snoop Doggy Dogg] called and said, 'I need some gear [clothes].' We took care of him and gave him great clothing, and he wore [our] rugby shirt on Saturday Night Live. The next day, everybody was looking for that shirt."[1]

Well, what God created for good, for fun, for love, and for ultimate gain inside your mind, Satan has become an expert at twisting, distorting, and eventually robbing from you. All that God intended for you to enjoy—especially regarding love and sex—Satan wants to corrupt.

As you read on, remember that if a word or a picture is put to music or clad in a lusty TV or movie scene, it sticks in one of those 10 billion rooms of your mind like Super Glue. If left unchecked, it will eventually cause you to think, say, and do things that you once never would have believed possible.

You want to know why millions of high-school and college students struggle with and fail at love and sex? Look who's dictating our morals!

Van Halen, a little old now but listened to for hours by millions over the last 15 years, says, "We celebrate all the sex and violence of television. That's Van Halen. I'm on the job to exercise all my sexual fantasies. When I'm on stage, it's like doing it with 20,000 of your closest friends."[2] *Broadcasting Magazine* enumerated the size of Van Halen's party by counting over 65,000 episodes of sexual behavior or reference to it during prime-time programming on NBC, ABC, and CBS in one season.[3]

Another teenager gets date-raped. Another boy loses control.

The group Slayer takes the message to the extreme, celebrating the "pleasures" of multiple rape.[4]

In a survey of 1,200 teenagers from all 50 states one recent summer, the group Nine Inch Nails was the second most popular artist/group. What are we thinking about? What are they saying to us? A line in one of their songs says, "I want to f___ you like an animal."[5]

Do you think their distorting influence bears some responsibility for the pain and disgrace of the 500,000 gonorrhea cases and 1,400 teenage AIDS cases that pop up each year?[6]

MTV's Tabitha Soren interviewed singer and songwriter

Ani DiFranco on *Week in Rock* and gave us a picture-window-sized view into MTV's heart.

> DiFranco: "I've fallen for girls before, and I've fallen for boys before. I write about it. It's all very out in the open."
>
> Soren: "Do you see someone's sexuality as changing throughout the years? Where do you stand at this moment? Or do you feel like you could go out with a guy or a girl now? Is it just like, depends on the night?"
>
> DiFranco: "Yeah. Make me an offer."
>
> Soren: "It sort of increases your odds."
>
> DiFranco: "Absolutely. I mean, I think it's hard enough to find somebody you can stand for more than 10 minutes, so like you shouldn't narrow your options."

You know what makes these mental manipulations even more unreasonable? Listening to rock music has now become the favorite activity among second-to-sixth-graders (66% say they enjoy it, compared to 59% for team sports and 47% for video games).[7] No wonder junior high is such a confusing time of life these days!

Are these people who get kids to empty their wallets to buy the latest CD civilized? Are they sane?

"When you go home, I want you to eat your parents!" says Billie Joe Armstrong of Green Day.[8]

Michael Jackson made $67 million in a recent two-year period. The Rolling Stones made $121 million. The Grateful Dead made $42 million.[9] They're getting rich, but by selling what?

Is it their drugs?

Pearl Jam's guitarist Stone Gossard: "I've certainly smoked [marijuana] every day for certain periods of my life. . . . I've abused it at times, but in general I'd say I enjoy it in moderation."[10]

Is it poetry?

Tabitha Soren interviewed AC/DC on MTV's *Week in Rock* and asked about the band's offensive lyrics. One of the band members said, "I like sex." Later, he added, "We're sexists." And then he said, "It's poetry. It's pure poetry."[11]

I *die* inside when I counsel a brokenhearted teenage girl or a boy whose dreams have been shattered by the actions of a musically indulged society. Their pain comes through each time I open a letter like this one:

Janet

The thing I regret most in my life would have to be losing my virginity. I was so young, and most people don't think 12-year-olds (7th grade) even know about sex. But I did and he did. We really didn't think it was all that wrong. I got my first kiss and lost my virginity all on the same day.

Is it sheer insanity?

Guns 'N Roses describes God's gift of wedded purity decadently. In the song "Used to Love Her," they repeat the line over and over, "I used to love her but I had to kill her."[12]

Is it numbness, like a brain full of Novocain?

As if preteens, barely teens, and the rest of MTV's audience needed to hear how "wonderful" the movie *Showgirls* is, the network interviewed numerous viewers and got the following:

MTV: "How many breasts did you count in this film?"
Viewer 6:   "I think about 143, but I lost track about
              halfway through the movie."
Viewer 8:   "I mean, there was a lot of flesh and bones,
              but it was good entertainment."
Viewer 17: "Actually, it was hysterically funny. But I
              don't think it was supposed to be."
Viewer 19: "I cried with laughter. So in that respect, it
              was enjoyable."

Let me show you how far those musicians and MTV viewers, with their casual reference to 143 breasts flying by like con-
fetti being thrown in the air at a New Year's Eve party, have
moved away from God's standard. Here are His priceless words
about a woman's breasts and the tender, delicate subject of
pure, unadulterated sex:

> As a loving hind and a graceful doe,
>   let her breasts satisfy you at all times;
>   be exhilarated always with her love. (Proverbs 5:19)

> How beautiful you arc, my darling,
>   how beautiful you are! . . .
> Your two breasts are like two fawns,
>   twins of a gazelle,
>   which feed among the lilies. . . .
> How beautiful and how delightful you are,
>   my love, with all your charms! . . .
> Oh, may your breasts be like clusters of the vine, . . .
>   and your mouth like the best wine! (Song of Solomon
>   4:1, 5; 7:6, 8-9)

Girls, God didn't intend for your features to be jeered at, abused, and destroyed by the selfish vices of the media and entertainment giants. This is *very* sacred territory.

Guys, your mind can be your greatest friend and your most important sex organ, *or* it will become your greatest enemy, betray you, and steal the intimacy of your marriage bed.

As for MTV, the record labels, and the artists who abuse the music industry through lyrics and images to the point of mental pornography, is it the drugs; is it greed; is it insanity; is it warped poetry; is it mental paralysis? On the surface, it's all the above. But to get to the heart of it, the Bible says it's all the work of Satan, the ultimate liar, the ultimate perverter, the ultimate counterfeiter of light.

The Bible calls him Lucifer, which means "light of brightness," because he always makes it *look so good, sound so cool, smell so inviting,* and *taste so sweet.* He is the master of deception. He'll make you fight to defend your territory if he has won your heart toward indecent music, MTV, TV, or movies.

Here's who he is, according to your Creator:

1. *Devil* (John 8:44) means the "accuser and slanderer." By calling him this, God is saying that Satan makes a false accusation against another; Satan's aim is to harm God and man; Satan will tell lies of any kind to achieve his ends.

2. *Satan* (Matthew 12:26) means "the resister or adversary." By calling him this, God is saying Satan reigns over a kingdom of darkness organized in opposition to God.

3. *Tempter* (Matthew 4:3) denotes that he seeks to lead men into sin, because he himself is a sinner. He tempts men by promising them, as a reward for disobeying God, delights or earthly power.

4. *Father of lies* (John 8:44) indicates that he is not just a liar, he is the originator of lies. He hates what God loves and loves what God hates.

5. *The one who holds the power of death* (Hebrews 2:14) tells us his ultimate aim is the destruction of our eternal souls.

6. *Beelzebul* (Mark 3:22-23) ascribes to the enemy a name meaning lord of the dunghill" or "lord of the flies."

7. *Belial* (2 Corinthians 6:15) means "worthlessness, wickedness," and "enemy."

8. *Evil one* (1 John 2:13) indicates that he is the supreme evildoer.

9. *Ruler of this world* (John 14:30); this title should give us some idea of the tremendous scope of Satan's power and activity on the earth.

Does what I've said in this chapter mean that all music and TV are evil? No. Michael W. Smith, dc Talk, Amy Grant, Audio Adrenaline, and many others are great personal friends. I know them well: their families, their lifestyles, their hearts. None of them wear halos, but they *all* seek to live godly lives and sing to bring out the best in people. TV is struggling to produce shows that will sell ad time but are also clean and pure. The decent shows are rare, but there are some. You just have to be extremely discerning and respectful of your mind and its ability to capture sights and sounds and never let go of them.

I'd like to tell you a story to close this difficult chapter, but I need to preface it by saying that if you'll guard your mind the way you'll someday guard your own children from evil or abuse, you'll know *every time* what music, TV, movies, and so on are okay and which are not.

I have two daughters, and they're my greatest treasures on planet Earth. I adore them, cherish their friendship, and stand in awe of my responsibility as their father.

When it came time for my oldest, Jamie, to begin to date, as you can imagine, I approached the first phone call from an aspiring teenage boy with great caution.

That call came one Thursday evening in April. "Hello, is Jamie there?" said the shaky adolescent voice on the other end.

Chills ran up my spine. The hand that held the receiver quickly became limp and clammy. I worked in vain to masquerade my nervousness. "Maybe," I said. "Who's speaking?"

"Uh . . . this is Josh, sir."

I had met Josh once. One of the local high-school kids told me he was thinking about asking Jamie to the prom. Josh was 6'4" tall, the center on our high-school basketball team. Why couldn't Jamie attract the attention of someone more my size? I thought. *How in the world, at age 44, could I look a giant in the eyes and get his attention properly if he mistreated my Princess?*

"What do you need, Josh?" The awkward conversation continued.

"Well, sir, I was, like, sorta wondering if maybe I might, like, ask Jamie to the prom or something."

It had happened. The teddy bears had faded and lost their furry toy-store texture. The fast forward button had been on for 15 years, and as hard as I tried, I couldn't find the pause button. She was 5'6" tall and as lovely and solid as the woman I'd loved for 18 of the best years of my life. Now David had Goliath on the phone, and I was grabbing for stones to load in my tiny slingshot.

"Well, Josh, how 'bout slipping by the house one of these days, and let's you and I have a little visit about this date."

"Do I have to?" he asked, his voice cracking.

"Sure, I think that would be appropriate. I'd like to meet you first and talk over some details of the evening together."

"Uh, I don't want to go out *that* bad," he blundered, as I'm sure I would have had I been in his shoes.

"Josh, you're 6'4" tall. You weigh 220 pounds. You're the starting center on the basketball team. Surely you're big enough to come over and speak to a shriveled-up old man, aren't you?"

"Uh, okay, sir. I'll be over tomorrow at 5:00."

I *did* want to talk about the date, but more than that, I wanted to have some fun. This was an opportunity I wouldn't let pass into the ordinary for anything.

About 30 minutes before Josh was to arrive, Jamie and I set the video camera up in some trees, pointing toward our front door. When Josh came to the door, he would be met by two of my good friends and fellow workers at our sports camp.

Stephan Moore is a handsome African-American basketball player from Arkansas. At 6'9" tall, he looked like a world-class Secret Service agent dressed in a black suit with dark sunglasses.

John Dickerson is a soldier *par excellence*; the commander of the corps of cadets from Texas A&M University. Dressed in field artillery gear, armed with a deer rifle, and wearing a camouflage-painted face, J. D. looked fit for guerrilla warfare.

With my two hit men staunchly "guarding" my front door, we were ready for the arrival of the high-school senior coming to request a date for the prom.

Roll camera.

Josh walked confidently down the pathway to my house, as predicted. Stephan and John stepped forward to meet him.

"Josh!" Stephan's deep, booming voice stopped the teenager in his tracks. "I hear you want to go to the prom with Jamie."

"Uh," Josh managed to say, gulping air. "Yes, sir. I was hoping to ask her dad about that, sir."

"Well, you've got to get by us first, because Jamie's like my little sister."

"Wow, I didn't know that . . . sir."

"Are you going to touch her?" Stephan shouted.

"Uh, no . . . no, sir," Josh stammered.

"How you goin' to escort her then?"

"Uh, I never thought about that, sir."

The interrogation went on for about five minutes as Jamie and I watched from the bushes, holding our sides and covering our mouths to refrain from bursting out with laughter.

Just before Josh's knees buckled, I stepped out and rescued the lad. We walked inside and joked about the hidden camera. Josh assured me that he'd bring Jamie home *early*. I gave him my consent. (I felt sorry for him!)

What sticks out most in my mind about the serious side of my conversation with Josh is that he chose Jamie as his date because he respected her. Funny thing—that's exactly why I chose her mom some 18 years before.

"Guard your heart," the Bible says. Get out your rifle and your two "biggest and baddest" friends! It's the only mind you'll ever have! It will belong to God, or it will belong to Satan. It's your choice, and the prize will go to the one to whom you choose to give your eyes, ears, and thoughts.

Controversial Issues

Baywatch, Melrose Place, Beverly Hills 90210, NYPD Blue, Donahue, Geraldo, MTV, Penthouse, Rolling Stone, Seventeen, and even *USA Today* have all waltzed far away from the basic principles God designed when He invented words like *love* and *happiness*. As if in a bad dream, we've almost forgotten what the original portrait looked like when He painted it with artistic perfection.

An eleventh-grader from Dallas named Rachel describes the confusion: "AIDS? It's kind of a joke, because none of our friends have it. . . . At the [small, private] school I used to go to, we had pools among ourselves to pay for abortions. . . . The more they [adults] preach to us about sex and alcohol, the more we're going to do it. . . . I do whatever my friends do to fit in. We had keg parties this summer; I was crawling around on the floor, walking into glass doors."[1]

What's right? What's wrong? Are condoms safe? Is abortion

just another form of birth control? Is homosexuality just another form of natural sexual expression?

With a lot of input from America's high-school students, I'll take on these controversial issues in the next few chapters and seek to tell you "the rest of the story" the mass media never communicate.

Condoms

The school board meeting was fiery the night we had a city-wide gathering to consider whether the high-school health clinic should pass out condoms to those requesting them.

Parental consent is required for the dispensing of aspirin. Yet in some states, abortions and condoms can be given without breathing a word to Mom or Dad. Hmm.

Anyway, after many girls and guys had told me through the years about the incredible sexual pressure kids are under nowadays, and how the presence of a condom on a date increases that pressure 10 times, to protect the girls in our school and enlighten the boys, I spoke to the assembly for a few heated minutes. The next day, the board voted "no dice" to the condom crime. Here are some of the facts on condoms that I presented that night (sorry, Planned Parenthood):

1. The AIDS virus is so small (0.1 mm) that it can potentially penetrate any standard condom.[2]
2. Slippage and breakage of condoms is 26 percent.[3]
3. Fifty percent of women who have abortions were using condoms or other forms of birth control.[4]
4. 32 percent of tested couples experienced condom slippage or breakage over a 16-day study period.[5]

And here's the clincher that they never tell you in health class: Condoms fail 100 *percent* of the time . . .

in protecting a boy's or girl's virginity.

in protecting a girl's reputation.

in protecting a boy's complex sexual memory bank.

in protecting a girl's or boy's relationship with Christ.

in protecting a couple's purity and friendship development.

in protecting a boy's respect for a girl and vice versa.

in protecting a girl's or boy's delicate self-image.

Finally, to put the nail in the coffin of condom mania, let me tell you candidly, as a married man, that once you begin to play Russian roulette with sex and to protect yourself and your partner from previously encountered disease with condoms, you are committing yourself to them for life. Condoms immensely dilute the pleasure of sex in marriage for both the man and the woman.

God intended sex to be natural, unspoiled, unprotected, unhampered by guilt, uncomplicated by fear, and protected for life by heterosexual, monogamous, husband-wife relationships. And He meant it to be the best.

Abortion

A young woman once told me, "I'm a third-grade teacher, and today was the first day of school. My students are eight and nine years old.

"The most awful thing that has ever happened in my life happened today as my new students walked into my class.

"You see, eight years ago, I had an abortion. My baby should have been one of my students today, but he'll never have that chance. I knew my abortion was wrong, but today it hit me just how wrong it really was."

The woman who told me that is a good friend. She's about as attractive as any girl I've ever met—and she attracted a promiscuous boy when she was in high school. They had sex; she became pregnant (like 3,000 other teenage girls that same day[6]); she elected to terminate the life of the baby (like 400,000 other teens that year[7]), and she cried for a long, long time (like almost all the 400,000 other teens did that year).

When two people have sex, a baby (whose life begins in a matter of seconds) is a natural result. But our "new society," with condoms on every street corner and sex by the hour in television and music, has produced 3 million teenagers with sexually transmitted diseases every year.[8] And of the million teenagers who get pregnant each year, 40 percent choose to end the baby's life by abortion.[9]

Did you know that:

1. More babies are killed by abortion in the United States each year than all the American soldiers who've ever died in all our wars since America began?[10]

2. An unborn child has his own fingers and toes after only six weeks?[11]

3. An unborn child has his own heart, his own blood, his own nervous system, and his own skeletal system? *None* of these is attached to the mom. He is all his own. His mom's womb is there to protect him and feed him.

4. An unborn child is *protected by law* from murder, but not from abortion? (Sound inexplicable and paradoxical to you?) In last week's newspaper, a man was charged with manslaughter for causing the death of an unborn baby, while U.S. abortion clinics killed 21 babies in the same second under the protection of the law![12]

5. 42.6 percent of teenage moms who undergo abortions suffer some kind of damage to their reproductive organs; 74 percent suffer incomplete operations and subsequent passage of the baby's body parts and tissue?[13]

6. 61 percent of Americans believe that abortion is morally wrong?[14]

7. Tampering with an eagle or hawk embryo in an egg can result in a fine or imprisonment, but *doctors get rich* by tampering with unborn human babies?

What word describes your emotions when you hear these facts? *Numb? Surprised? Angry? Upset? Disbelieving? Grieved? Sickened? Sad? Confused? Indifferent?*

Which term would you use to describe abortion? *Medical procedure? Fetal interruption? Murder? Pregnancy termination? Genocide?*

If you were asleep in your house at midnight and an armed burglar broke in through your bedroom window, and before you could wake up to defend yourself he shot and killed you, which term would you use to describe the event? *Home-entering procedure? Somnia interruption? Sleep termination? Murder?*

The Bible is clear on the moment when life begins. Consider the following examples:

In Genesis 4:1, God specifically connected the birth of Eve's son Cain to his conception.

In Job 3:3, Job—a great man of God—connected his birth directly to the night of his conception: "Let the day perish on which I *was to be born,* and the night which said, 'A boy is conceived'" (emphasis added). The Hebrew word for *boy* used in this text specifically applies to the preborn human being.

Luke 1:41 and 44 graphically describe the "fetus" of John the Baptist as fully human: "And it came about that when Elizabeth heard Mary's greeting, the *baby* leaped in her womb; and Elizabeth was filled with the Holy Spirit" (Luke 1:41, emphasis added).

"For behold, when the sound of your greeting reached my

ears, the *baby* leaped in my womb for joy" (Luke 1:44, emphasis added).

The word for *baby* in the original Greek manuscript of those verses is the same word used for "baby Jesus" in Luke 2:12, when He lay in the manger on the night of His birth.

It should be fulfilling for you to know that God likewise gave *you* personal life from the night of your conception.

Check out this fatherly expression of love from God to you in Psalm 139:13-16:

> For Thou didst form my inward parts; Thou didst weave me *in my mother's womb.* I will give thanks to Thee, for I am fearfully and wonderfully made; wonderful are Thy works, and my soul knows it very well. My frame was not hidden from Thee, when I was made in secret, and skillfully wrought in the depths of the earth. Thine eyes have seen my unformed substance; and in Thy book they were all written, the days that were ordained for me, when as yet there was not one of them. (emphasis added)

Prayerfully consider these biblical passages as well:

"Listen to Me, O islands, and pay attention, you peoples from afar. The Lord called Me from the womb; from the body of My mother He named Me" (Isaiah 49:1).

"Before I formed you in the womb I knew you, and before you were born I consecrated you; I have appointed you a prophet to the nations" (Jeremiah 1:5).

"But he said to me, 'Behold, you shall conceive and give birth to a son, and now you shall not drink wine or strong drink nor eat any unclean thing, for the boy shall be a Nazirite to God *from the womb to the day of his death'*" (Judges 13:7, emphasis added).

Believe it or not, pro-choice (pro-abortion) people use the following arguments to justify abortions:

1. "He's not a child until he has a name."
2. "He's not a child until he breathes air."
3. "A baby evolves in the womb and sort of goes through the 'fish stage,' the 'reptile stage,' and the 'monkey stage' of evolution before he actually becomes a baby."
4. "The baby really isn't an individual. He's not his own person. He doesn't belong to God; he is his mom's personal property to do with as she wills." (Imagine what our country would be like if parents could kill their children at any age whenever they chose.)

Don't you feel fortunate that your mom and mine listened to their hearts, listened to God, fulfilled their calling, and didn't have us terminated before we were able to protest?

A precious girl named Gianna Jessen lived through her mother's attempt to abort her, and now at age 18, she lives to tell how thankful she is that she's alive and well and her mother's abortion failed to kill her.

Speaking at a Mother's Day banquet at a church, Gianna explained, "I'm adopted. My biological mother was 17 when I was born. At seven months pregnant, she chose to have a saline abortion. But by the grace of God, I survived. I forgive her totally for what she did. She was young, and she probably had no hope. She didn't know what she was doing. As a result of the abortion, however, I have cerebral palsy—but that's okay, because I have God to keep me going every day. It's not always easy, but He is always there. He's there for you, too." She finished by singing Michael W. Smith's "Friends," dedicating it to all the babies who die from abortion every day. "They are my friends," Gianna said, "and I'm going to see them in heaven someday."[15]

If you've had an abortion, go to a forgiving God and ask for forgiveness. "If we confess our sins, He is faithful and righteous to forgive us our sins and to cleanse us from all unrighteousness" (1 John 1:9). And please, go see a qualified Christian counselor and work through it as soon as you can. Yes, God's love is big enough to reach around any broken and repentant heart. *He can heal yours, too.*

My dear friend Annie became pregnant out of wedlock. She was first surprised, then mad, then ashamed, and finally she came to her senses. Two friends advised her to have an abortion. Her parents wisely counseled her to deliver the baby and give it up for adoption. She moved away from home to gallantly spend a tough nine months to finish the job she had begun. Annie interviewed several couples who desired that baby as much as their own lives! At last, she selected "the perfect home" and gave the baby away. I called her after the delivery, and she was smiling as she cried happy tears.

"Yes, I'm okay," she reassured me. "If you could have seen the look of wonder on that precious mom and dad's faces when I gave them the baby, you never would have needed to worry. That look of appreciation will comfort me forever."

In Romans 8:28, God gave us one of His most incredible promises when He said, "And we know that God causes all things to work together for good to those who love God, to those who are called according to His purpose." Here is just one more true story of how real His Word is:

Sally

My sophomore year, my sister came home and told us she was pregnant. She wasn't married, either. At first she wanted to get an abortion, then she decided to give it up for adoption. At last she decided to marry the guy and keep the kid.

This last decision proved to be the best because both my sister and brother-in-law are awesome Christians. They realized they had made a mistake, and they asked forgiveness from each other and from God. From that moment on, they became totally different people. I am happy to say that with the support of both sets of families and God, my sister and brother-in-law have been married for two wonderful years. Their daughter is the most precious thing in their lives now! (She is in mine, too.)

I feel this incident proves that with the support of God, things that seem like burdens or mistakes can be turned into the best things in your life.

How Gay Is Gay?

Richard's dad was never home. Actually, Richard liked him better when he wasn't. His mom was domineering and critical. He was more talented in music and the fine arts than he was in football or basketball. Making male friends was tough. He never felt accepted by "the guys." Because he seemed effeminate to the guys, the popular girls also rejected him. In junior high, his puberty was about all he had for pleasure.

Then in eighth grade, along came a high-school kid named Billy. Yes, he was openly gay, but at least he was caring and accepting. Billy told Richard that gay was just another expression of his sexuality and no worse than looking at a *Penthouse* magazine or "fooling around" with a girl. Richard wanted to go to his dad with his questions about his feelings for Billy, but his dad would have killed him. Within two years, Richard had joined the discreet high-school gay club and accepted that lifestyle as his way of finding friends.

But inside, he was dying.

He drank on weekends to kill the pain. Suicide was constantly on his mind. He didn't worry about getting AIDS, because he figured death might be his best alternative.

His church gave him an uncertain picture of right and wrong in this area. *USA Today* and NBC News supported his new lifestyle with encouraging stories about fellow gays and the progress they were making. The TV sitcoms and soaps showed gay couples that actually looked very happy.

Why, then, he often asked himself, did he feel as if his problems were continually escalating? Why did he feel so cruddy inside? Why did he want to die?

The above scenario is true, many times over. The details differ from case to case, but many of the symptoms are similar. Homosexuality and lesbianism have been around for centuries. They're definitely a part of society today. My camp colleagues and I have met with many through the years. One of those I counseled wrote me this insightful letter:

> Gay is not good, nor is it a happy way to live. The very people who claimed they were happy where they were at, on a deeper level of communication, admitted they were miserable and had the lowest self-esteem later on. These people who claimed they were happy being gay were actually more miserable than the people who said they were miserable being gay! I talked to well over 200 individuals, and there were no exceptions to this. I myself fit into both categories at one time or another. Any homosexual—

even if he doesn't admit it to anyone but himself—
wishes that he were something other than what he
has let himself become.

Although the current trend of politically correct media
would lead you to believe that the homosexual lifestyle is safe
and emotionally stable, the facts sadly and tragically disagree.

- 43 percent of homosexuals say they have had more than
  (get this) 500 sexual partners in their lifetime.[16]
- 28 percent of white gays have had more than 1,000
  sexual partners in their lifetime.[17]
- Only one out of 100 gays has had fewer than four
  sexual partners in his lifetime.[18]

Gays also have to deal with the problem of sexually transmitted diseases that unnatural sex propagates. The 38 painful,
sometimes deadly sexually transmitted diseases that plague our
sexually active American society are at their peak in the gay
community.

- 35 to 40 percent of the gay males in San Francisco are
  estimated to be HIV-infected.[19]
- 45 to 55 percent of the Los Angeles homosexual community is estimated to be HIV-infected.[20]
- Up to 100 percent of HIV-infected individuals could
  eventually die of AIDS or related conditions.[21]

No wonder the Bible is so clear when it condemns the
practice of homosexuality in these three passages:

"Or do you not know that the unrighteous shall not
inherit the kingdom of God? Do not be deceived; neither fornicators, nor idolaters, nor adulterers, nor effeminate, nor
homosexuals, nor thieves, nor the covetous, nor drunkards,
nor revilers, nor swindlers, shall inherit the kingdom of God"
(1 Corinthians 6:9-10).

"For this reason God gave them over to degrading passions; for their women exchanged the natural function for that which is unnatural, and in the same way also the men abandoned the natural function of the woman and burned in their desire toward one another, men with men committing indecent acts and receiving in their own persons the due penalty of their error" (Romans 1:26-27).

"And God created man in His own image, in the image of God He created him; male and female He created them" (Genesis 1:27).

The statistics are startlingly clear in showing that the further you get from God's plan of "one man, one woman, together forever," the more dire the consequences become. If homosexuality in your mind or in your actions is a problem for you, an outstanding, helpful book to read is *Desires in Conflict* by Joe Dallas.

Almost all solid Christian counselors agree that homosexuals and lesbians have *legitimate needs* for a strong father figure and solid friendships with peers. The gay lifestyle is an *illegitimate* way to meet those legitimate needs. Many gays are finding help and freedom today by trusting Christ to forgive them and show them legitimate ways to meet those needs. I highly recommend the Dallas book to you as you seek forgiveness and a way to return to God's best for your life. Remember that God hates the sins of homosexual lust and conduct, just as He hates all sins, but He loves the sinner who seeks Him with his whole heart.

A King to Fit the Crown

A NOVEL

As far back as I can remember, there had been a shortage of kings at Stedman High School. Not that it caused a panic or a decline in enrollment, but there was an awkwardness at the annual homecoming coronation when the queen had to stand alone in front of the student body and receive her bouquet from Principal Fishbind with a handshake instead of from a king with a kiss. Naturally, fewer and fewer girls were willing to be nominated, and the growing opinion amongst the female half of the student body was that it didn't matter what kind of king they got for the position, just as long as they got one.

So it was that Stedman High became open to all kinds of potential kings: lazy kings, unruly kings, and kings who skipped class to smoke their fathers' cigarettes, stolen that morning and stashed in backpacks. When questioned about the lack of kings, however, the boys at Stedman High didn't care a thing about homecoming or whether they ever produced another king from their ranks. So, the crown remained untouched in the trophy case.

From where I sat at the librarian's desk with my two assistants, Daisy Bucket and Matt Ransom, I had a good view of the neglected ornament. It sat in the same place assigned to it 20 years earlier by a local jeweler whose name escapes me, but whose words I will never forget.

"The crown must fit the head! And the head must fit the neck! And the neck must fit the shoulders of the man who would be king!" growled the jeweler as he placed the crown in the trophy case. He was a bear of a man, and we were all a little afraid of him. But no one said anything negative about his work, for he had come highly recommended, and it was said of his masterpiece that it would especially sparkle when worn by just the right person.

It was a beautiful crown. Around its base were five stones, each of them standing for a virtue the jeweler said was essential to kingliness: an emerald for *character*, a diamond for *courage*, a blue sapphire for *vision*, a ruby for *reputation*, and a topaz for *influence*.

"These are the virtues of a good and godly king," the jeweler told us as the five words were being etched in the wall above the trophy case. "Without them, a kingdom might as well be governed by a poached egg."

Nevertheless, from the spot where the jeweler had gingerly placed it, the crown had not moved one inch, because in all the years since its creation, there had never been a boy who wanted to wear it—that is, until the morning lovely Donnamere Lake transferred from

Crosstown Girls' Preparatory School. Then every boy at
Stedman grew a sudden interest in how his head might
look with a crown on it.

One morning, I came upon a red-letter-jacketed senior
named Danny Lavender, who was lying on his back on the
floor with his calculator and compass, looking up through
the glass shelves. He was a real fashion plate if ever there
was one: perfect hair, perfect teeth, perfect tan on his perfect torso. I didn't care that he was the varsity quarterback.
He always had overdue library books, so I didn't trust him
any further than I could throw him.

"All right, Lavender," I said. "Move along. You're going
to be late for class."

Danny pressed his compass against the glass and traced
a circle, then pushed several buttons on his calculator and
looked up at me. "Come on, Miss Caraway, just 30 seconds more," he begged. "If anyone's head ought to fit this
stupid thing, mine ought to."

"Why all the rush to be king?" I asked.

"Man, Miss Caraway," replied Danny. "What planet
have you been living on?"

"Earth, last time I checked."

Danny sat up with an astonished look on his face.

"The rush to be king is about Donnamere Lake," he
said, extending upturned hands as if to draw some obvious
response from me.

I shrugged to show I had no idea who he was talking
about.

"You know," said Danny, "the girl from Crosstown,
the one who's up for homecoming queen."

"Ohh . . . *that* girl," I said. "I guess I haven't noticed
her yet."

"Haven't noticed her yet?" said Danny. "She's only the most gorgeous babe to ever set foot in this school."

Suddenly, I heard the sharp click of heels behind me, and I noticed Danny gawking over my shoulder.

"Good morning, Daniel," came the voice of an angel.

I turned to see a stunning, scarcely human swan of a girl gliding toward us on long, liquid legs. She stopped at Danny's feet and stood over him with her hands on her hips.

"I said, *Good morning*," she repeated impatiently.

Danny's eyes were round with wonder. "Goog merdnon," he said.

"Why are you on the floor?" the girl inquired. "Have you lost something?"

Danny tried to sit up, but his arms failed him. "Me worz just clerking at the rown," he burbled.

"I think what he's trying to say is that he's on his way to class," I offered.

"He sounds like he's on his way to the psycho ward," said the girl.

I reached out to shake her hand. "You must be . . ."

"Donnamere Lake," she replied, obviously in love with the sound of her name. She ignored my hand and made a dramatic toss of her golden locks.

"I don't believe we've met," I said.

"Haven't we?" said Donnamere. "I see you all the time in the library. By the way, I love your hair."

"Thank you," I said, quickly checking my appearance in the trophy case.

"You know," continued Donnamere, "it's people like you who are responsible for bringing back whole fads. I

mean, who would have ever thought the beehive would
return?"

I decided then and there I wasn't going to vote for her.
"Young lady, don't you have someplace you ought to be?" I
demanded.

"I was on my way to drama," replied Donnamere
coolly. She looked at Danny, still tongue-tied on the floor.
"What is it with him, anyway?" she asked.

"He's a little shy," I told her.

"It seems like all the boys at Stedman are shy these
days," said Donnamere. She gave her hair another toss.

Inwardly, I yearned for the girl to deliver just one overdue book to me. "To class," I ordered, pointing down the
hall. "And don't be late."

Donnamere's eyebrows shot up like bright bird's wings,
and the two of us exchanged a cold nod. "Nice meeting
you," she said, stepping lightly over Danny Lavender and
disappearing in a cloud of perfume.

"Beehive my foot," I said. "Who does she think she is?
The Duchess of Yorkshire?"

"She's Donnamere Lake," said Danny, gazing after her.
"Did I tell you she's up for homecoming queen?"

I peered deep into Danny's eyes until a corner of his
mush-and-rainbow soul appeared. "You're nuts," I declared.

"Thanks for the input, Miss Caraway," said Danny,
standing to brush himself off. "But I really must be going
now. I've got a campaign to plan."

"Campaign?" I blurted. "Don't tell me there are others
who are interested in being king?"

Danny chuckled. "Guys have been giving away their
lunch tickets to be nominated."

I shook my head in disbelief. "When did all this happen?"

"When you were gone to that librarians' convention."

"A full-blown nomination was held?"

"Uh huh. We've got a candidate from every class."

"That's impossible. Nobody wants to be king."

"They do now," said Danny. He began to count the nominees on his fingers. "Robert Scheister III from the sophomores, Tom Sykes from the juniors, and yours truly," he concluded, jabbing a thumb at his chest. "I'm going to win the whole thing."

Here, I must pause to tell you that with a short list like that, a victory for Danny Lavender was not entirely out of the question. Robert Scheister III had only recently been caught with a rat he had stolen from the physiology lab, trying to duct tape the unlucky creature inside a classmate's locker. By a stroke of luck, Dr. Fishbind happened to be patrolling the halls that morning when he heard a shrill squeak. Upon catching young Scheister red-handed, he suspended him for 10 days. The rat was returned to its cage, where it huddled, trembling, for weeks, until it finally died and was put into a time capsule and buried.

Regarding Tom Sykes, there is nothing much to say except that he once drove a Harley-Davidson through the building and ran out of gas in front of Dr. Fishbind's office. Tom was not a very bright boy.

After my initial encounter with Donnamere, I began to notice an evil theme in the hallway conversations of Stedman High. It was a tradition of sorts, this theme which had reappeared like crabgrass for the last four years. It always brought a dead feeling to the bottom of my stomach.

"Daisy Bucket's up for queen," went the phrase, followed by snickers and snide remarks.

"Why, Daisy's not that bad," someone would say, covering his mouth and trying hard not to laugh. "In fact, I like old Daisy. Of course, I like a good skin rash now and then, too. But that doesn't change the way I feel about her."

Such laughter would follow that I was sure it would reach the ears of the poor girl who had served me for years, indexing books and periodicals. Daisy Bucket was a kind person and as dependable as one can be who is confined to a wheelchair. She would have been tall if not for her condition. Her clothes were several fads behind the fashion, and her hair, though always clean and combed, was of an unremarkable color. Besides the wheelchair, the most noticeable feature about Daisy was her crooked teeth. So crooked were they that several of the meaner boys took great delight in calling her Daisy Bucktooth instead of Daisy Bucket. But there was a far greater pain that Daisy had to endure throughout her education at Stedman High.

Every year at homecoming, someone would nominate Daisy for queen, and every year she would receive only one solitary vote. Ten thousand theories existed about the identity of Daisy's secret admirer, and these theories became the topic at a dozen different lunch tables every day in the cafeteria. No admirer ever materialized, though. And gradually, the light in Daisy's eyes grew dimmer and dimmer, until all that was left was a mere shadow of anticipation.

Now, I was fortunate to have another faithful assistant as well, one whose personality and presence brightened my days. One morning, while sitting at the checkout desk, I happened to glance over at Matt Ransom, and I noticed he was gazing through the open library doors to a place in the hallway where Robert Scheister III had begun his own campaign for king.

"Hello, sister!" Robert called to a girl who was loaded with books. "I'll carry your stuff for you if you don't mind me bending your ear a bit."

The girl eyed Robert, appearing at first as if she might steer around him and be on her way. She had heard the rumors of him and the rat.

"Trust me," crooned Robert, grinning broadly.

The girl wavered for a moment. Overcome with her heavy load, however, she reluctantly gave in to his offer.

"That's the ticket," said Robert, snatching her books. "By the way, you may not have known this," he began as they started off toward the girl's class, "but I was recently nominated for homecoming king, and I surely would appreciate you casting your vote for Robert P. Scheister III. You know, for a long time I've been thinking that the schools with greater candidate participation are the schools that . . ."

I watched until the two of them disappeared in the mass of bodies and I could no longer hear their voices.

"Interesting character," said Matt, snapping a rubber band around a stack of catalog cards.

I set my elbows in a rectangle of warm sunlight on the desk and rested my chin in my hands. "Matt?" I said with a sideways glance at my assistant.

"Hmm?"

"Have you ever thought of running for king?" I asked.

"No," said Matt.

"I could arrange for you to be nominated."

"I'm not the type they're looking for."

"But if there was ever an example of character and courage and vision and—"

"Thank you," interrupted Matt without looking up from his work.

I shifted my chin and stared at the handsome, black-haired young man. He was broad in the shoulders, which suited him well in his position at fullback on the Stedman Steelers football team. Some said it was he, not Danny Lavender, who could take credit for the previous year's championship victory. Such a claim would never come from Matt's lips, though. He was generally too busy study-ing or helping others make it through Mr. Dilfer's chem-istry class to care much about his athletic accomplishments. Matt was going to be a doctor someday, and to that end he devoted most of his energy.

"She's going to get her heart broken again," I said, moving my attention to the back of the library, where Daisy was taking books from a cart and stacking them on the shelves.

"She might," said Matt. "But she'll probably get one vote, too. That always seems to cheer her up until Febru-ary."

"Right," I said. "Just in time for some jerk to send her a box of Valentine's candy with a frog inside."

Matt looked away, and I could see that his shoulders were shaking slightly.

"What's so funny?" I asked.

"You've got to admit it was humorous when that frog jumped out in Daisy's lap last year," Matt replied.

"It was not," I insisted. "It was mean and cruel, and whoever did it should have been expelled forever."

"Lighten up, Miss Caraway," Matt said. "A few hard knocks never hurt anybody."

"Matthew Ransom!" I exclaimed. "How could you say

such a thing? That girl has had more than her share of hard knocks. How would *you* like to be in her shoes?"

Matt grew suddenly serious. "I just think she'll be a stronger person because of it, that's all," he said quietly.

Hot anger raced up my neck and face. Fortunately, there were not many students in the library at that hour, so I unleashed my full wrath on Matt. "You of all people!" I shouted. "Here I always thought you were good and kind and . . . and all those other things written up there on that wall," I said, pointing toward the trophy case. "But you're just as bad as the others!"

Matt lowered his head, and the two of us did not speak to each other for the rest of that morning.

Meanwhile, the campaign for king was developing into a dogfight. Tom Sykes decided that Robert Scheister III could tote all the books he wanted. As for himself, he'd get his votes by hanging out in the library, gaining the favor of that one segment of school population he had always hated most—namely, freshmen. Every day, I would see Tom performing at least one out-of-character deed aimed at winning the coveted kiss from Donnamere. Sometimes he would roam about the tables, asking if anybody needed a pencil sharpened. Other times, he would check papers for spelling errors or look up books for someone's bibliography.

However, as I mentioned before, Tom Sykes was not a very bright boy, so the vote-getting method he eventually settled upon was good, old-fashioned terrorism. Soon, Tom had a comfortable lead in the polls, and ninth-graders who had not pledged their allegiance to him sported either a black eye or a set of Harley tracks across their parents' front yard.

Election day grew nearer. With only two weeks left
until the votes were cast, I was surprised that Danny Lavender had not yet made his move. Another candidate had
entered the race for queen by way of a late nomination.
Her name was Elizabeth Rothchild, and she was the perfect
picture of snobbery, though her features paled in compari-
son to Donnamere Lake's. Matt and I were still at odds. He
seemed preoccupied with the whisperings of students who
came to the library often and sat in dark, out-of-the-way
tables, mourning the upcoming finals. Soon, these secret
conversations reached my desk in bits and pieces.

"Dilfer's test is going to be a doozer," said one informant.

"Yeah, and nobody but that brain Ransom has ever
passed the thing," said another.

As each woeful student approached me, I scolded him
or her with the same advice. "Maybe you ought to spend
more time studying for the test than talking about how
hard it's going to be," I said. But no matter how much I
urged them to prepare themselves, the fear of flunking
chemistry could not be overcome.

Reginald Dilfer was a bald man who, in his spare time,
had been working on a hair-growth tonic, for which he
hoped to win a Nobel Prize. In short, he was a frustrated
scientist whose exams were known to be cruel and
unusual. This year, they would be murder because Reginald Dilfer was far from finished with his invention and,
consequently, more irritable than ever at finals.

One day, after the most recent recipient of my scold-
ing trudged off to lament his doom, Matt Ransom came
up behind me and tapped me on the shoulder.

"Hey," he said, managing a sort of peace-offering
smile.

"Hey yourself, stranger," I replied. I followed with an easy topic for both of us. "One more game before homecoming, I guess. Who is it this weekend? Henrietta?"

"Yep," said Matt.

"I hear the Hens are supposed to be a pushover."

"Maybe. Maybe not," replied Matt. He studied me for a moment, choosing his words carefully. "It doesn't sound like Dilfer's chemistry test is going to be a pushover," he said finally.

"It won't be if people don't develop some courage and start taking it seriously," I replied.

"Why should they?" said Matt.

I was caught off guard by his nonchalance. "What do you mean, why should they? That's what students are supposed to do in school."

"Not if they know where they can get the answers to the test."

I froze. "What test are you talking about?" I asked.

"Mr. Dilfer's," said Matt. "I overheard some guys saying that Danny Lavender got a key to the chem lab and plans to break in next Wednesday evening after practice. He's going to steal the test and sell it to anyone who's willing to pay his price."

"Let me guess," I said, holding up a trembling hand to interrupt Matt. "One test in exchange for one vote."

"That's right," said Matt.

"But half the school is enrolled in that class," I estimated out loud.

Matt nodded. "Danny hopes Tom and Robert will split the other 50 percent of the votes."

"This Donnamere obsession has gone too far," I said

as I stepped around the corner of my desk and headed for Dr. Fishbind's office.

"Not so fast," said Matt, taking hold of my elbow.

"Now listen here, young man," I warned. "I've been the librarian at Stedman High for 27 years, and I'm not about to lose my job over some lovesick prankster."

A tiny sparkle came to Matt's eye, and he put a finger to his lips. "Listen," he said, "I have a plan. I know something about old Dilfer's hair goo that no one else knows."

I sat down in my chair, and Matt proceeded to reveal his plan, all the while glancing around to see if anyone was eavesdropping. When he was finished, I could hardly wait for the following Wednesday.

But Matt's plan never got off the ground—at least not with him present to oversee its success. The news of his injury at the Henrietta game fell upon Stedman High like a lonely, shriveled, wrinkled balloon. I was at home with my cat and needlepoint when the telephone rang. Poor Daisy Bucket's voice came leaking through the receiver.

"Wait a minute, now. Slow down, sweetheart," I adjured her. "I can barely understand you when you're talking like that. There, there. That's better. Now, what was it you were saying about the Henrietta game?"

Five minutes later, I was watching the reruns on the 10 o'clock sports. They showed the collision a half-dozen times, from a half-dozen different angles. I sat there motionless on my sofa as the paramedics carried Matt off the field to the waiting ambulance. "Paralyzed from the waist down," the sports announcer speculated. I must have repeated those words a hundred times that weekend, each time with a wag of my disbelieving head.

Monday morning, the campaign for king was back in full gear, and the rumor of Danny Lavender's impending burglary grew to epic size. By Wednesday evening, every student enrolled in Mr. Dilfer's chemistry class held his or her breath in hopes that the rumor would become a reality. Danny didn't let them down.

Thursday's finals came and went like a lamb. Reginald Dilfer was beside himself when he graded the test and discovered 95 percent of his class had scored in the genius level. "It can't be!" I heard him shouting clear down at the other end of the hall. "This is the hardest test I've ever given, and they've made it look like kindergarten material! I must be losing it!" he cried. If I remember correctly, Reginald took the rest of that day off and even missed the homecoming assembly.

After the exams, the halls were filled with students pressing toward the ballot boxes. When the voting was over, the boxes were whisked away for tabulation, and the great, wide doors of the auditorium were opened to the curious throng. In we squeezed to await the announcement of the royal family. It was not hard to guess who had won the election. I only hoped Daisy would take it well.

Under hot lights, the empty stage itself seemed to sweat as it waited impatiently for the contestants to take their places. There were five chairs in all: one for each of the nominees representing his or her respective class, plus a taped-off spot for Daisy's wheelchair.

Tom and Daisy were the first to enter at the back of the room. I had prayed that by some miracle, Daisy would appear radiant for the event. Instead, she seemed more terrified than ever. To make matters worse, Tom Sykes in a tuxedo looked as out of place as a rat in a cat factory. In record time, he executed his escort duties, rolling Daisy unceremoniously down the center aisle, up the handicap ramp on the left side of the stage, and to her designated spot. Immediately, a dull laughter began, and I watched Daisy wilt under the cruelty of her peers.

Next came Robert Scheister III and Elizabeth. They were not a bad-looking couple, as crooks and snobs go.

Finally, a hush fell over the auditorium, and every head in the room turned simultaneously, as if connected to a universal hinge. Donnamere Lake had made her entrance. She wore a silk dress, primarily of autumn colors, with an enormous bow on her backside, the effect of which—in my opinion—made her look like a turkey bewitched to a golden brown. She was actually quite beautiful, but her comment about my beehive hairdo still irked me. Behind her, by at least 10 feet, walked Danny Lavender, the hero of every chemistry student. I remember noting that his baseball cap seemed ill-suited for such an occasion, and that he didn't look or act at all herolike. When all the nominees were assembled on the stage, Dr. Fishbind and Mayor Brown stood and walked to the podium.

A thousand seconds must have passed while Mayor Brown opened the envelope and stared at its contents. At last, he gripped the microphone and announced the results.

They were as expected.

Donnamere blushed with mock embarrassment when the mayor handed her the victory orchids. I will be the first to say that she did look lovely as a queen, even though her heart was black with conceit. However, when the crown was placed upon Danny Lavender's head, not one of its five jewels sparkled. Instead, he stood there like a codfish with his mouth open, as nonsparkling as can be.

At that point, Elizabeth Rothchild fell all to pieces. She smacked Robert Scheister III in the nose with her runner-up bouquet and stormed off the stage, screaming things too colorful to repeat in this story. Robert winced in pain, while the new king and queen shoved past him to the spot at the center stage that was marked with a masking-tape X. From where I sat, I could see Tom Sykes's dull expression and Daisy's hands poised firmly on the wheels of her wheelchair. She couldn't wait to get out of there, back to the library and the familiarity of nobodyness.

The traditional kiss was an unnecessarily long one, so long, in fact, that I wondered if either of the participants might need to come up for air. Just as the clinch was being broken off by Dr. Fishbind, something amazing happened. Encumbered by the weight of the crown, Danny's baseball cap tilted backward, then plummeted to the floor. He scrambled to retrieve it, but not quickly enough.

"He's bald!" someone gasped.

Indeed, he was—slick bald, without a single shred of fuzz to conceal the fact that Danny Lavender had stolen a whole lot more than an examination key on that infamous Wednesday night. Matt's words in the library came whizzing back to me with new meaning: *"I know something about old Dilfer's hair goo that no one else knows."* On the heels of this recollection came another one: *"The crown must fit the head, and the head must fit the neck, and the neck must fit the shoulders of the man who would be king.*"

At once, I knew the secret of Danny's baldness. He had stolen Dilfer's hair tonic to make his head fit the crown.

For a moment, Danny faced the audience and tried to appear calm. His charade lasted about seven seconds. With a shriek of humiliation, he bolted stage left, but not without hooking the hem of Donnamere's dress with his shoe and taking a large chunk of it with him.

Queen Donnamere was mortified. Immediately, she flung her orchids on the floor and fled along the same path that Elizabeth Rothchild had taken, straight from the auditorium and out the front door, never to be seen at Stedman High again.

Meanwhile, the mass exodus of royalty had left two bewildered escorts and a trembling flower of a girl to face an entire auditorium.

"Do something," I heard Mayor Brown order no one in particular.

A large woman from the German department, Ms. Beluga, stood up in the audience. "I think the runner-up is supposed to be granted the position of queen," she suggested.

"May I remind you that our runner-up is probably in the ladies' room throwing a tantrum," said Dr. Fishbind somewhat sharply.

"Then that leaves Daisy," said Ms. Beluga. "How many votes did Daisy get?"

It was deathly still in the room. All eyes looked at Dr.

Fishbind, who had been the official tallier of votes. He glanced at Daisy and lowered his head. "She didn't receive any," he said quietly.

A lump came to my throat as I watched Daisy's shoulders slump. Not a single vote? No secret admirer? I wondered if this would be the final blow to her fragile self-esteem. Suddenly, there was a noise at the back of the auditorium, followed by a clear, familiar voice.

"She receives one now," the voice said.

I whirled around and saw Matt Ransom . . . in a *wheelchair!* He was dressed in a white tuxedo and flanked by two nurses from the local hospital. Slowly, painfully, he progressed down the aisle. When he reached the ramp and one of the nurses offered her help, he shook his head and fixed his eyes on Daisy. All by himself, he ascended the stage and came alongside the perplexed girl. He took her hand and kissed it.

"I believe we have a queen," he announced.

I could contain myself no longer.

"Three cheers for Queen Daisy!" I shouted, beginning to applaud. Soon others joined me, and then the entire room erupted in praise.

Mayor Brown wiped his forehead. "Is there a king to go with our queen?" he asked.

"Without a doubt," replied Dr. Fishbind. He quickly retrieved the crown from the spot where Danny had dumped it. For a moment, he paused to look at Tom Sykes and Robert P. Scheister III. They both took a half step forward.

"Stand aside, gentlemen," said Dr. Fishbind, bypassing Tom and Robert and walking directly to Matt's wheelchair. "I'm embarrassed to say that for four years, character and courage and vision and reputation and influence have existed right under our noses, and we never even acknowledged it. I can think of no better person to wear this." And then he placed the crown on Matt's head.

The jewels in Matt's crown began to wink and sparkle. He took Daisy's hand and raised it high. If there was a dry eye in the room, I didn't see it. My own were too flooded with tears to even notice our newly elected king and queen as they worked their way back up the auditorium aisle and out into the brightness of the hallway.

The rest of that week was a blur. Even without Matt Ransom at fullback, the underdog Stedman Steelers won our homecoming game by a landslide. Perhaps we rode to victory on the enthusiasm of the crowd. Perhaps Danny Lavender was a step quicker without his hair. The Saturday *Morning News* called it the most dazzling display of power to ever grace the gridiron. If you ask me, I'd say we won because our hearts were changed.

Matt Ransom graduated that spring and went on to study dentistry at some university. I should also mention that Mr. Dilfer's hair tonic did eventually win a Nobel Prize, but not for its hair-producing capabilities. Instead, his product is known today as the world's most effective wart remover.

A year or two after I relinquished my post as librarian, I got a Christmas card and photo from a Dr. and Mrs. Matthew Ransom. The picture was graced by an indescribably beautiful young wife named Daisy Ransom, with a cover-girl smile, and around the edge was a border made out of five words.

CHARACTER.

COURAGE.

VISION.
REPUTATION.
INFLUENCE.

I smiled as I placed the card on my mantel. To this day, it remains there as a reminder of that miraculous November when Stedman High School finally found a king to fit the crown.

THE END

The Topaz ·······························

Influence

Jumbo shrimp
Date rape
Making love
Ugly sunset
Sweet 'n sour sauce
Sweet Tarts
Good whiskey
Happy tears
Icy hot

Oxymorons. They're hilarious when you think about them. How did two words so opposite in meaning get together in the first place?

The oxymoron that drives me nuts as I listen to kids with broken hearts is the term that I hear so often these days, "peer pressure."

A peer, defined, is *a friend.* A friend is someone you can depend on, lean on when times are tough; someone who brings out the best in you; someone who puts your needs ahead of his; someone you can trust.

Influence is how you affect the people around you. Influence is the crown jewel you give to your friends (good or bad) by the way you live your life every day.

By the same token, influence is how your friends find those same qualities demonstrated in you. Influence means they don't have to guard their hearts when you're around. Instead, your example enables them to open their hearts and let the sunshine of your life come flooding in.

You and I have read the surveys. We've heard the stories. Without a doubt, over 90 percent of the people who are hooked on drugs (or dead) were introduced to drugs by, guess who? A *friend.*

And tragic as it seems, almost 100 percent of the truly shattered hearts in dating relationships—where sex was taken, virginity was lost, abortions were encouraged, love was taken for granted, and promises were broken—were initiated by, yep, a boyfriend or girlfriend. It's horrible. But I can't point my finger. Without Christ and His grace, I'm as guilty as anyone.

These letters kids write to me continue to haunt me.

Margaret

Since I started dating, I have always promised myself that I would stay a virgin until I was married. I have lived up to that promise until the past year. He said that he loved me, and, like all the others, we would get married. I really believed he loved me. After our first time, I started taking the pill to keep from getting pregnant. Two months later, he dropped me for his old girlfriend (who was once pregnant by him). I felt as if I had 200 knives go through me. I was crushed.

The pain friends cause each other is unbelievable. Let me suggest a little filter to place over your heart to sift through *anyone's* character before you start to hang out together or listen to his or her ideas.

1. Does this person follow Christ and His Word?
2. Does this person *really* have my best interests at heart?
3. Does this person have wisdom and discernment? Does he or she have a keen sense of right and wrong?
4. Would this person ever betray me?
5. Is this person trying to use me to gain status for himself or herself?
6. Do my parents approve of this person? (This one is more important than you can imagine.)

Lynne

When I was 15, I lost my most precious gift that I had to a football player I didn't even know. My best friend had set us up. She told me she had lost hers to the very same guy. It's been about a year, and so far, I've willingly given myself to eight guys. I knew it was wrong, but I went ahead and did it anyway. I want to be happy and loved. I am so miserable because of what I've done. Why did my friend get me into this?

In contrast, "And the peace of God, which surpasses all comprehension, shall *guard your hearts* and your minds in Christ Jesus" (Philippians 4:7, emphasis added).

Here's a list of phrases of influence often used by manipulators to get the sex they want (in the left hand column), along with the phrases their victims often use after the fact (in the right-hand column):

Phrases of Influence: Before and After

Before	*After*
This is exactly . . .	I wish I would have . . .
It feels so right.	Why did I . . .
He is *sooooo* hot.	I should have . . .
She wants you to ask her.	If I'd only known . . .
You look so cute together.	It didn't start off like that.
This is gonna be great.	Why didn't he tell me?
Nobody will know.	But she looked so innocent.
But if you love me . . .	I just didn't think he would . . .
Let's try it for a while.	Why does it hurt so bad?
It'll be okay . . .	I can't believe I ever trusted . . .
Don't worry about it.	But it seemed so right.
But love covers a multitude of sins.	Why didn't somebody tell me . . .
Nobody's home.	I just can't forget.
This will give us security.	I feel so guilty.
We need something more . . .	Those memories . . .
Let's see what it's like.	Whatever happened to . . .
You try on shoes before you buy 'em, don't ya?	But you said . . .
Let's run over to my place for a minute.	It just doesn't feel the same anymore.
We'll get married someday.	But what am I going to do about . . .

Here's the "Top 10 List" of baloney "friendship phrases" I've picked up from guys and girls I've known—before and after the big event.

10. "I won't tell anybody."
9. "Let me tell ya about this guy that wants to take you out."
8. "Check her out, man. She is soooo hot!"
7. "What are you, chicken or something?"
6. "You're not *still* a virgin, are you?"
5. "Hey, that stuff went out with the Dark Ages, man."
4. (The Classic) "Hey, everybody's doing it."
3. "If you love me, you'll let me."
2. "You try on shoes before you buy 'em. It's just like sex. Give it a try. If it fits, wear it."
1. "Just this once!"

You've got to have your baloney detector up higher than a kite, don't you? It's as if you're in a submarine in enemy territory, and your periscope is always up, looking around for unfriendly vessels. When you spy one, you sure don't surface the ship, snuggle up to it, and say, "Hey, let's go sailing together." No, you push the torpedo button and run like crazy.

That's what Paul told Timothy (and you and me) when he said, "Flee from youthful lusts" (2 Timothy 2:22). It literally means to run for your life when you recognize the enemy—especially when he calls himself or herself a friend.

Stephanie

I met an older guy last year, and he was into pot and sex. I thought it was so cool going out with him. We got into a romantic interlude and began to mess around and smoke pot together. My mom questioned me about him, but I always lied about it. Once we were smoking a "J" in my room, and my mom smelled the smoke. He freaked! I lied again but got grounded forever. I wanted to kill everybody. I got sent away to a home. I thought I was in love with this guy. After I returned to my own home months later, I saw him after about a week; he barely even knew my name! I was crushed.

But influence can also be positive.

Kara

When my boyfriend and I became more serious, we had a talk about how far was too far for each of us. (Believe me, it wasn't simple, but the awkwardness put into perspective what an important issue it was, both personally and for our relationship.) However, my line of too far was not as far as his. After telling him why I felt this way, his mind wasn't changed.

Later that day, he came rushing over to my house to tell me how he had been thinking and had decided for himself what he felt was too far. After he had come from such a "whatever is comfortable for you is good for me" attitude, I could see the delight or feeling of relief or happiness that making a decision for himself had brought him. Making your decision before the moment is incredibly important, because decisions coming during a moment can't be thought out.

The Blue Sapphire ·

Vision

In junior high, her friends called her a "goodie-goodie cartoon freak." While the walls of their rooms were lined with posters of Michael Jackson, Tom Cruise, and Michael J. Fox, hers were adorned with pictures of Sebastian from *The Little Mermaid* and Rajah from *Aladdin*. Even in high school, the easygoing, uncomplicated girl with the big, brown eyes quietly maintained her G-rated life, content to stay home on weekends while her friends dated, partied, and "had all the fun."

She knew how other girls "got the cute guys." She certainly turned boys' heads more than once, but in their right mind, they wouldn't want to ask out a girl who was this straight and offered no hope for anything physical or a good time at a party. The only dried flowers in her room were a corsage or two from a rare prom date and a vase of dried red roses given one at a time, on special occasions, by her sentimental dad, who loved her like no one else on earth. She was the apple of his eye and the little girl who had fulfilled his life's greatest dream.

And so the naive, brown-eyed girl graduated from high school just the way she planned it—heart intact, no regrets, free from the "chains of high-school romance," and ready for college. You see, this girl had a vision. She wanted one true love, the kind of love that lasts a lifetime, with the man that God had prepared for her since the beginning of time.

As the G-rated girl went to college, her dreams grew dim. Her roommates and friends went on many dates to sorority and fraternity functions, football games, and weekend trips. But she didn't compromise her standards and held on to her dream with all her might. Her greatest qualities were loyalty and faithfulness as she stayed committed to her God, her family, and her "someday husband to be."

During her freshman year, in one of her classes, she met a guy. He was a dedicated student but stayed busy on weekends dating several beautiful girls, as he was considered the "best catch" in the freshman class. As the weeks passed, the handsome lad and the brown-eyed girl developed a rich friendship. Though they never went on dates or became romantically attracted, they talked, laughed, and played when they weren't too busy with school or he wasn't on a date. The G-rated girl continued her pattern of contentment, loyalty, and devotion. Her vision remained true.

After a year and three months of quality friendship-building with picnics, walks in the park, and road trips to wherever, the boy asked the girl to his family's old home in Indiana, where his grandparents lived. Once there, after listening to family stories for a while, the two college friends went up to the attic to admire some heirlooms. They laughed at old pictures and antique memories, and then the boy looked at the one who had become the best friend he had ever known, and he grew very quiet.

He looked down into the faithful, brown eyes and, with sober conviction, told her, "Jamie, I think you've stolen my heart, and I'll never get it back again." Then he leaned down and kissed her gently on the lips. It was only the second boy's kiss she had ever experienced.

Jamie returned to her home a few days later, found me (yes, I'm her dad), and told me the whole wonderful story. As she walked carefully through the storybook details, dozens of tears welled up inside me and ran down my cheeks like a silent stream, for I had prayed for her and her lifetime love thousands upon thousands of times since she was a tiny toddler 19 years before.

Vision is the magic that gives a dream staying power. Vision fills with hope all the yeses you say to yourself when your chin is down. Vision envelops with solidarity all the no's you say to would-be vision stealers. Vision gets you out of bed on Monday morning with a smile and gives you a desire to press on. Vision takes your courage and points it to the finish line.

Tonight, as I write, will be a night that I will never forget. In less than 12 hours, I'll be in the grandstands, cheering (but probably crying quietly inside).

Tonight, a lifelong dream will come true. But like most dreams, this one definitely came the hard way. Let me explain.

Brady was gentle, frail, and nonathletic. He was the perfect candidate for ridicule on the park-board soccer team that introduced him to the world of competitive athletics.

From age six until third grade, he was the laughingstock of the team. He couldn't walk and kick the ball. His teammates would send him home in tears, poking fun at his name, "Brady Bunch, Brady Bunch, couldn't kick a ball at lunch."

I had a habit, as a new dad, of lying by my kids at night and talking through the day. I'll never forget the night the greatest friendship I'll ever know began. Brady was sobbing on his pillow.

"Dad, why do they pick on me like that?" he asked.

"I dunno, Son, but one thing's for sure. I'm crazy about you, and I couldn't care less if you ever play sports again as long as you live. You might be an artist or a guitar player or—"

"But Dad, I want to play sports!"

"Well," I reassured him, "you can do anything you want

to, if you want it bad enough. And . . . Buddy . . . there's nothing I'd like more than to help you get there."

"You would? I can? Do you mean it?" His teary eyes were filled with hope.

"Brady, make a goal, and we'll dream the dream together."

"I'd like to play in the NBA."

I immediately wished he'd said anything but basketball. Five guys on the floor and the whole school watching is a formula for failure 99 percent of the time. But I stammered, "Uh, okay. Why don't you pick a goal a little closer at hand that you could achieve in the next three or four years?"

"Dad," he said, looking up at me with wonder and trust as only a child can, "I'd like to start as point guard on the seventh-grade basketball team."

I groaned inside but somehow knew that "all things are possible to him who believes."

"Okay, Buddy," I said, "but we'll have to work out together every day after school for the next four years."

Though that fateful night came in like a dark cloud of hopelessness, God was in the cloud, beginning a father-son friendship that would travel far beyond my wildest dreams.

We ran; we dribbled; we shot; we did push-ups; we sweated; we cried; we stepped on each other's toes; we trained; we memorized Scripture; we prayed. We discovered friendship.

I'll never forget the smile on his face as he dribbled the ball down the court to usher in his seventh-grade basketball season just the way he had dreamed it. I was so nervous that I had to leave the gym to pray for courage. The game was tied with four minutes left. He threw the ball away twice in a row and missed a free throw, as his team lost by one. He was crushed, but I poured out encouragement.

It was a rough year, but for the first time in his life, Brady tasted accomplishment.

Our times together intensified. He continued to climb. I continued to encourage. He was the dreamer. I was a dream-maker.

The peers were hard on him in junior high.

His little brother and I were his only male friends.

Going into ninth grade, he shot over 60,000 baskets. I stood under the net and caught over half of them. Countless nights after work, I'd come home, and we'd drive around town to find a gym and a kind janitor who'd let us in to shoot for an hour or two.

His ninth-grade year, it finally all began to come together. Though still far from perfection, he played well, handled the ball well, played good defense, and scored lots of points. His team went 19-0, his peers finally accepted him, and his gentle spirit began to be appreciated. Though he plays for a public school, his entire team comes to the house every Thursday morning for doughnuts and Bible study.

His elusive dream was still to start on the high-school varsity squad. He made just under 5,000 three-point shots in the month of October as he put the final polish on his first chance to reach his dream. And now, the night I spoke of at the beginning of this story, he will be in the starting varsity lineup, and that long-awaited dream will finally come true.

The difference between vision and a fairy tale or a pipe dream is the conviction it takes to turn the vision into real, tangible goals, the goals into action plans, and the action plans into memories—memories that fill your scrapbook . . . memories that no one but *no one* can ever take away.

Here's another example of what I mean.

Neal Jeffrey is a great buddy who stuttered so badly that he could hardly make a sentence in his first 12 years of school. His vision was to be an NFL quarterback. The problem was, he was slow, short, and couldn't call a play in the huddle. His goal was to throw 200 to 300 passes every day. His action plan was to come straight home from school, pick up his football, and throw until his goal was reached.

In high school, his passes hit the receivers' hands with uncanny accuracy. The coach ran each play onto the field with a wide receiver. The receiver would call the play in the huddle. On the line of scrimmage, Neal put his hands under the center and smiled at the defense. The fullback called the cadence. Down-set-hut-hut-hut.

Neal's vision carried him to Baylor University, where he not only was the starting quarterback, but he also led the Bears to the Cotton Bowl and their first Southwest Conference Championship in many years. The Southwest Conference has gone into the annals of football history, but Neal's vision will never be forgotten.

Neal went on to play with the San Diego Chargers, and though occasional stuttering still makes him and his audience smile, Neal has learned that his gift, of all things, is teaching. Now he leads people around America to reach for life's higher goals, like the one God gave him in his first vision of Gods' calling.

Of the 1,200 teenagers from 50 states and five continents who attended our summer camps one recent year, a full 85 percent said in a confidential survey that they were virgins (boys and girls included). Over 90 percent of those who were virgins had set a firm goal to stay virgin until marriage, and

73 percent of those proposed to keep their morals pure by staying completely alcohol free.

Solid goals give vision grit. If a guy has a vision to be fascinated by his wife as long as he lives, for instance, he had better have a goal to stay completely away from pornography, passionate relationships, and revealing movies or his mind as a married man will be cluttered with confusing and distracting pictures of extramarital experiences. Goals make sense out of vision.

Vision is one of the greatest jewels in the crown of character. Praying for and establishing your vision today would be one of the most valuable decisions you'll ever make.

A 16-year-old friend named Rob shared a story with me that captures his vision for sexual purity in a way that will never let him down.

Rob

My sister got married two weeks ago, and I saw the most beautiful and happiest marriage in my entire life. My sister is very close to God, and in her few relationships in college and in high school, she put God first. Last year, she met the neatest Christian man that had the same morals she did about Christianity. You had to be there to see the joy on their faces because they saved the purity of their bodies for their whole life for that day. I want that joy on my wedding day, and I want to look my wife in the face on that day and say, "I love you and God so much that I saved my sexual purity for when it was meant to be, which is now." I look up to my sister for her strength and her love for God. I pray that someday I can have the same joy she had a week ago.

The Ruby ···

Reputation

I met a girl at Southern Methodist University during my college football days more than a few years ago. A cheerleader, she always brought the crowd to its feet as she led our team into the stadium doing round-off back handsprings across the Astroturf. Debbie-Jo was probably the poorest girl at SMU. After losing her dad in a plane crash when she was four, her family of five kids struggled just to keep the bills paid. But even though she couldn't shop at Neiman Marcus like many other SMU girls, Debbie-Jo came to class each day in the finest designer clothes you ever laid your eyes on.

Seventeen magazine and *Mademoiselle* would have dispatched photographers to Dallas daily if their magazines could fathom the depth of her true beauty. Though their camera lenses would only have seen faded jeans and workout clothes, the "threads" I noticed on her were the fibers of her unquestionable reputation. Reputation is how you really look. It's how you dress yourself every day—not in cotton, silk, or nylon threads, but in the lifestyle that attracts men's or ladies' hearts (not just their eyes). I'll never forget calling Debbie-Jo for the first time during her junior year at the Kappa Alpha Theta sorority house, where she lived. Her roommate answered the phone and let me know that Debbie-Jo was at a party with the Sigma Alpha Epsilon fraternity. I asked her roommate if Debbie-Jo would be drinking, and to my *amazement* her roommate replied as if shocked, "Definitely not. Debbie-Jo never drinks."

No wonder guys and girls at SMU respected her so. No

wonder so many guys would have given anything to develop a real relationship with her. No wonder I "fell over dead" for her. No wonder she continues to be more intimately attractive to me with each passing year! No wonder her two daughters are so much like her!

I define *reputation* as how the people you care about the most would describe you. The three primary issues that affect your reputation as a young person are alcohol, drugs, and sex. I believe this story by a 14-year-old girl I met one recent summer describes it best:

Lissa

During my eighth-grade year, I had a very low self-esteem. All my friends were turning to drinking, and I thought that alcohol was a bad trap to be in, so I secluded myself from those people and was very lonely. I joined a school play group and became interested in a guy in the play. I found out that he was a heavy drinker, and though I had stood my ground for over six months, I turned to heavy drinking. After a while, he became interested in me, or what I had become. I allowed myself to become whatever anyone thought I was. As a result, I became known as "easy" or a slut. I hadn't done anything at that point to live up to that title. One of my guy friends brought this to my attention, and from then on I went downhill, engaging in many physical activities with different guys. Now I walk through halls and hear songs of ridicule. I am ashamed of myself, and even my sister and closest friend think I am trash.

A high-school newspaper called the *Westside Glance* featured an article titled "S.C.A.M." that uncovered the mystery of why the guys and girls who wear the *real* designer clothes (a first-class reputation) are rare commodities in our sexy world.

Scam, described by Westside students as a "casual sexual relationship with no commitment," can spell problems and pain for many teenagers.

To some, "scamming" is a sure way to get hurt. "Girls are more often taken advantage of," Barb Goeser, senior, said. "If a guy scams a lot, everyone thinks he's a stud. If a girl scams a lot, everyone thinks she's a whore. It's a real double standard," she said. Goeser said that if each person involved in the relationship would "keep their mouth shut," no one would be taken advantage of or hurt.

"It's just good, clean fun at the time," Steve Laird, junior, said. "Later on, or the next day at school it gets to be a problem. The girl feels taken advantage of," Laird said.

Most people scam because they "don't want the relationship and just want the action," Terry Beutler, senior, said.

"Scamming is bad," Shannon Donaldson, senior, said. "It shows that you have no respect for the other person and no respect for yourself."

"The problem with scamming is that everyone knows about what the girl does Monday at school," Debbie Koory, junior, said.

"Scamming can be good or bad," Jim Simon, senior, said. "Someone can get hurt, but it's a good way to have a sexual relationship without making a serious commitment. In high school, it's important to have fun, and for a lot of people, scamming is just a way to have a good time."[1]

The cartoon presented with the article says it all:

The tragedy about the flippant attitude toward someone's reputation is that someday everyone, and I mean *everyone*, will care. There's no double standard in regard to reputation. I've seen the most oblivious "studs" in high school become the most conscientious fathers on earth. *They would give everything* for a clean reputation before their wives and kids. Don't be deceived! If anything, we men need to raise a higher standard and really *take the lead* in building and protecting a girl's reputation. A college boy named Mark was sharp enough to know the ruby in this truth!

Mark was dating a young woman named Mary. He had made a commitment to never go beyond kissing before marriage. At night when he'd come home from his dates with Mary, his roommate, John, would question him about the physical side of the relationship. Mark would always tell John the same story: "John, we only kiss. That's the way it's going to be. I want her honeymoon and marriage to be pure and guilt-free, whether it's me she marries or someone else."

John would poke fun at Mark in a way that only college roommates can do. But Mark held his ground.

As the months went by, Mark and Mary decided to break up and remain "just friends" for a lifetime.

Guess who began dating Mary after that? You guessed it— John. They dated, fell in love, and were married.

Guess who John's best man was? You guessed it again— Mark.

After a wonderful wedding, John put his arm around Mark and, with tears of gratitude in his eyes, said to his best friend, "Mark, I used to kid you about being so pure with Mary. But buddy, I can never thank you enough for treating her like you did. I owe you more than you'll ever know."

Do you want to wear the most desirable "clothes" every day the rest of your life? Well, toss the tight sweater and suggestive jeans, and slip into some threads that will look really hot—especially when the day of days comes and you walk down the wedding aisle into the arms of the man or woman of your dreams.

Here are some guidelines to help you do that:

1. Establish your standard. Write it down. Aim low and you'll hit it every time. Aim high and walk with the best "dressers" in the land.

2. Share your standard with someone who really cares about you, and ask the person to hold you accountable to your goal.

3. Select good friends to hang out with. You *are* who you're with. "Bad company corrupts good morals" (1 Corinthians 15:33).

4. Stay a million miles away from drugs and alcohol. As my 15-year-old friend Chad said, "Alcohol and drugs begin to control you. They get to your head and make you do things you never would have considered doing."

5. Be careful with music, TV, and movies. If you see it or think about it enough, eventually it gets in your blood.

6. Don't go alone to the house or room of anyone of the opposite sex. Date rape, seduction, and mere rumor leave countless victims with tattered reputations every day.

7. Become an expert at saying no. When someone asks you to drink, tell 'em you don't look good in a lampshade (and smile). When someone tries to force sex, tell 'em your dad is a Green Beret and trains Dobermans for a living.

8. Build a friendship, not a sexual partnership. If someone isn't interested in you without the physical, he or she is not after love but sex and is not worth gambling your reputation on.

9. If someone gossips about others to you, they'll gossip to others about you. Choose your conversations wisely.

10. What goes around, comes around. Protect your date's reputation and he or she will be more likely to protect yours. And who knows—you may start a positive trend at your school!

The Diamond

Courage

Spartan soldiers, though never noted for their flattery, have been admired for centuries for their matchless courage on the field of battle.

Around 350 B.C., when the Greek Empire was the strongest power on earth, Philip of Macedonia sought to conquer and subdue the Spartan people. Philip brought a huge army to their border and issued a decree that stated, "If you do not submit at once, I will invade your country. And if I invade, I will pillage and burn everything you hold dear. If I march into Laconia, I will level your great city to the ground."

The Spartans sent Philip their brief and typically blunt reply. Philip's eyes narrowed in anger as he read their one-word challenge: "If."[2]

"If"—that was it. You can fill in the blanks yourself. Imagine all the challenges that surrounded their one-word answer. "If you're bad enough!" "If you're as tough as you think you are." "If you wanna get smoked." "If you fight as tough as you talk."

Saying "If" to the Macedonians is like a 17-year-old boy or girl in the crucible of sexual pressure saying no.

Saying "If" to the general of the world's greatest army takes courage.

Saying no to the ruler of darkness and his scheme to dethrone you from God's plan for a kingly or queenly reign as blissfully, sexually married takes equal courage.

It took great courage for my 17-year-old friend Lisa to fight off a "street man" when she was attacked brutally. Her face and hip were broken in an attempted rape, but with the help of a dear woman who heard her cries for help, Lisa, at all of 116 pounds, held off the intruder.

It took equal courage for Monica to break up with her boyfriend after giving her heart to Christ last summer at camp. He was the heartthrob of almost every girl in school; he had become her security blanket. In many ways, in fact, he had become her idol, and they had engaged in sex many times. But now, Monica knew she was "a new creation in Christ." For five tearful days, we talked about "counting the cost" of turning to Christ. She knew she must choose God (and her own long-range good) or Shane (and her immediate pleasure).

After great deliberation, her courage won, and she chose God.

It took equal courage and perhaps even greater fortitude for a young man I've known for years to take his girlfriend to her home night after night until they were married. She felt that sex was acceptable before marriage. He didn't. Their honeymoon was their first time together. To Travis, love wasn't something you "made," it was something that grew inside two people's hearts over the course of a lifetime.

Courage. A fine stone in the crown of a young champion.

My courageous oldest brother, Bob, has always been one of my dearest heroes. He has cherished, admired, and served the only love he's ever known since he married her 30 years ago. His wife, Mary Evelyn, developed kidney failure not long ago, and her condition worsened so quickly that in a matter of days, her unfiltered blood rendered her dead on the charts and medical standards. A donor kidney was not available with an exact match to her tissue type. Her plight looked hopeless until Bob asked to have his kidney tested for compatibility.

Miraculously, his (though about two times the size of hers) matched perfectly. Quickly, the surgeons rushed the two lovebirds into the operating room. He came out with a missing kidney and three ribs and some back and side pain that will be his "love reminder" until he dies. She came out with a filtering system that works flawlessly. He laughs at his pain. She'll probably outlive him. He would have given her his heart if that was what she needed.

The Emerald ·······································

Character

Character is what you do when nobody else is looking. Whereas reputation is how other people would describe you, character is how God would. Whereas vision makes you a good "human doing," character makes you a good "human being." Character says no to wrongdoing and puts muscle behind it.

A 17-year-old unmarried mother came to a friend of mine seeking advice. The girl was hurting badly, her tears had been many, and she couldn't "go it" alone. She had failed to "flee the temptation."

During her junior year in high school, she met a guy who was everything a girl could ask for. He was the most popular boy in school; he was cute; he was a talented athlete. But his reputation with girls was bad. He prided himself in always getting what he wanted on a date.

She was attracted to him but turned off by his reputation. Two weeks went by, and she got the phone call. He asked her to a movie. A little red flag went up in her mind.

 Flag No. 1 (Say "No")

10 seconds

Her emotions were calm; she had 10 seconds to say no. She rationalized, "There will be lots of people there. Maybe I can help him. Okay, I'll go."

He picked her up as planned. She stayed on her side of the car. As they passed the theater, he said, "I've seen that show; it's boring. Let's go to the beach. There're lots of kids down there, and we can play some volleyball and stuff."

The second red flag went up in her mind.

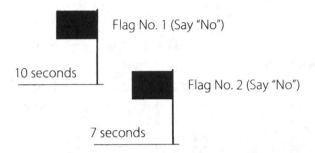

Flag No. 1 (Say "No")

10 seconds

Flag No. 2 (Say "No")

7 seconds

She again felt in control and rationalized that with all the kids around, there would be no problems. She said, "Let's go."

When they got to the beach, no one else was there. He said, "Wow, the party must have moved. Let's just talk a little while."

The third flag went up.

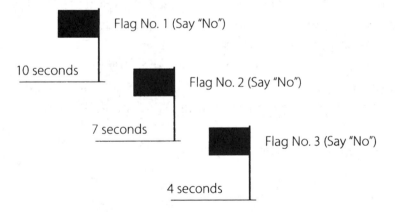

Flag No. 1 (Say "No")

10 seconds

Flag No. 2 (Say "No")

7 seconds

Flag No. 3 (Say "No")

4 seconds

She found it harder and harder to say no. She had less time to make decisions, and the pressure was growing. She agreed to stay. After 30 minutes of chatter, he moved over to her side of the seat. He calmly put his arm around her shoulders and began to "make his moves" to arouse her emotions.

The fourth red flag went up in her mind and was big and easy to see.

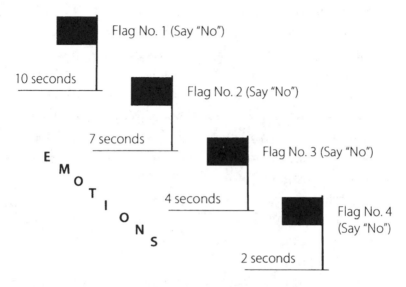

The flags kept flying. She kept giving in. Nine months later, she gave birth to an unwanted, fatherless baby. Character gives you the strength to stand on your own two feet and *do* what you *know is* the right thing.

Johnny Ferrier is a "Hero Forever" at our sports camps. He was loved by everyone. He was a fine athlete, America's "Top Gun" fighter pilot, father of three awesome kids—Johnny had it all. (His best gift was definitely his character.) One day in a giant air show, to the amazement of half a million viewers, as Johnny acrobatically flew his Sabre jet, the steering mechanism locked up. His commanding officer repeatedly ordered Johnny to bail out. Johnny refused the order and, with brute strength, manually guided the plane into a backyard garden, the only open spot he could find in a heavily populated community. Nobody was hurt but Johnny. He died on impact. No one who knew Johnny well was surprised by his last heroic deed.

His character had always guided him to do what he knew was right, no matter what personal sacrifice it entailed.

Shannon Marketic is like a daughter to me. We've been close friends for years. I've always admired her character. As a teenager, at the urging of friends and family, she entered the Miss California pageant. Before a panel of liberal and politically correct judges, Shannon was asked who her hero was. She looked steadily into their eyes and said, "Jesus Christ." Expecting a much more hardline feminist viewpoint, the judges pressed for another answer. Shannon responded, "Next to Jesus, it would have to be my dad."

She won the crown. The judges were criticized for giving the crown to an outspoken Christian. One judge responded, "Well, she was the only candidate who knew what she stood for and wouldn't back down."

At the Miss USA Pageant, she had two chances to give more "popular" answers to difficult questions. She again stuck to her convictions, knowing that character was more important than a crown.

Again, she won the title.

After her year as Miss USA was over, Hollywood rushed to her with millions of dollars worth of movie roles to perform. They all had sexual themes. She refused them all. For five years, Shannon and her family have been *broke*. They could have used the money. The last chapter of her book hasn't been written, but when it is, her character will be spelled out on every page.

Andy Ellett is the point guard of our local high-school basketball team and the quarterback of our football team. Once a week, he helps me lead eight of his buddies in a Bible study. Every Friday morning, he leads the Fellowship of Christian Athletes meeting of 40-50 students. His goal is to walk his talk and leave a legacy of Christian example in the high school. I've heard him pray many times. His prayers often include time to ask God to bless his future wife, whoever and wherever she is. Andy Ellett is not a world-class athlete. He does, however, have world-class character.

USA Today loves to shock us with all the terrible "teen statistics" and horror stories of teens killing each other, holding up stores, getting drunk, raping, and committing suicide. Never do they report the thousands of teenagers and college students I've met from New York to California who are saying,

"No, thanks, I don't drink."

"No, thanks, I don't go to that kind of movie."

"No, thanks, I won't be going to that party."

"Maybe I'd better take you home; things might get a little out of hand if we kiss any longer."

"I'd rather protect your purity than satisfy my pleasure."

"No, thanks, I can't go out with you. I'm busy with family that night."

Yes, American morality may be sliding, but the reason we won World War I and World War II and continue to amaze the world with our strength is that amidst all the crime and selfish, hedonistic, headline-grabbing living, there are men and women of character in this country as in no other nation on earth.

I still cherish the letter of great character I received from a teenage friend named Jenni. Jenni knows what makes true love grow.

Jenni

I told Matt that anything other than kissing before marriage was wrong. He told me that he didn't care what we did or didn't do, he would always love me

because of the special person I am. I told him that as
much as I loved and cared for him, trying to please
him, that Jesus still always came first. He agreed
and said we should definitely put Christ as the center
of our relationship. Isn't that great? God is <u>so</u> awesome! He really answers my prayers—always. I've
been praying so hard (this is my first "true love"), and
I was so confused. I've heard of millions of Christians
slipping and going the wrong way, and I just didn't
want that to happen to me. My relationship with the
Lord is too important to me for me to jeopardize it.

Character is definitely one of the most prized jewels in the
"crown of success" that any person, young or old, will ever
wear.

Lou Holtz has won many football games at Arkansas and
Notre Dame. His offensive coordinator and I hang out a lot
and laugh about crazy football stories. Lou's right-hand assistant
told me once that at the team's first fall meeting, he tells the
players, "All right, guys, there are only two rules around here:
1. Do what's right. 2. Don't do what's wrong. Any questions?"

There are never any questions.

Every time you say no when everybody else is wrongly saying yes, you develop character.

Every time you put someone else's needs above your wants,
you develop character.

Every time you put God first in your life, you develop
character.

Every time you ask "What would Jesus do?" when faced
with a tough decision, you develop character.

Character makes great athletes, great wives, great hus-
bands, great moms and dads, great leaders, great team cap-

tains, great girlfriends and boyfriends, and most importantly, great witnesses for Christ.

A recent letter from an 18-year-old guy named Dennis says it all:

Dennis

Something has been troubling me lately. My girl-friend, Shelly, wants to make love, and I'm not ready. She said she's ready, but I want to save my body for my wife, my first love, not my girlfriend or my friends. But she doesn't realize that yet, and I'm try-ing to talk to her. I've told her no and that I'm not ready, but she keeps telling me that we can do it one time and if I don't like it, we won't do it again. But I know it only takes one time to get her pregnant, and that is not what I want. Besides, the Bible tells me no, too. So I hope she comes to and realizes that we can't do it. And I promise you that I will not ever make love until I know it's right, and that's with my wife (when I find the person who is right for me).

The Perfect Guest

If there's one verse in all of God's Word that fills my sails with speed-propelling wind like no other, it would have to be, "The Lord is not slow about His promise, as some count slowness, but is patient toward you, not wishing for any to perish but for all to come to repentance" (2 Peter 3:9). You know what that means? God wants *you* to be in His family! The way He accomplishes that is to give you the grace to open the greatest Christmas gift you'll ever be able to touch with your own hands.

To make this most-important-of-all chapters clear, I offer some pictures. The Bible identifies three kinds of people.

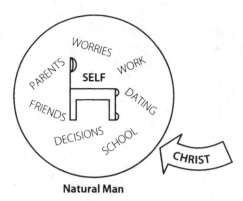

Natural Man

1. The throne pictured here is the throne of your life. Whoever sits on it calls the shots. He's in control, and all areas of life revolve around him. This life is usually characterized by searching, guilt, confusion, and loneliness.

First Corinthians 2:14 says, "[A] natural man does not accept the things of the Spirit of God; for they are foolishness to him."

Spiritual Man

2. Here, Christ has been invited into the life. The Holy Spirit now has been placed in control, and He gives the person strength and power over the areas of his life. (This life is characterized by love, happiness, and peaceful feelings.)

Jesus said, "I am come that they might have life, and that they might have it more abundantly" (John 10:10, KJV). He not only adds years to your life, but He adds life to your years. He came not only for the sweet by and by, but also for the nasty here and now.

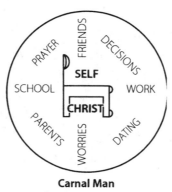

Carnal Man

3. Here, the Holy Spirit is in the life, but self is back on the throne. Most of the decisions are made to gratify self. Christ is resident, but He's not president. (This life is characterized by an up-and-down spiritual and emotional existence.)

I believe that once a person sincerely gives his heart to Jesus, He is there forever. But if this "carnal man" picture is you, you need to ask, "Did I really, sincerely give my life to Him in the first place, or was I just saying the words of a prayer that had no life-changing meaning to me?" If you are practicing habitual sin, and that fact doesn't bother you, read Romans 6, 7, and 8, and give your heart completely to the Savior!

Which of these represents you, and which would you like to be? If number two (spiritual man) is your goal, you can expect your smile to grow. Your ability to love and be loved will become greater.

Here's why:

When you become a Christian, the Perfect Guest (the Holy Spirit) comes into your life. When Christ went to "sit at the right hand to judge the nations," His Spirit was given to the earth to bring people happiness, satisfaction, and power for holy living.

The Holy Spirit is a "helper" to give you peaceful feelings.

The Holy Spirit is the "comforter" to give you loving feelings.

The Holy Spirit is "power" to give you the ability to do what you know is right.

To be a spiritual person, you need to ask God to control every area of your life and to be your Lord. Then, by faith, thank Him for doing it.

"Ask, and you will receive" (John 16:24). Is God a liar? I know He's not.

"Lord, fill me with Your Spirit. I give my life to You."

After years of trying to do it all myself, I found I had achieved all my goals except one. I was unhappy. I didn't know anything about love, particularly in terms of sex. I finally gave my life to Jesus. The "Perfect Guest" came into my home, and what a difference He made in my life!

Now almost every day, I get to watch Christ change another person's life. I watch Him remove guilt from so many young people who've made mistakes and want to turn around. I've seen kids pray in desperation before or after a suicide attempt, and that self-destructive desire was replaced with a desire to live, love, and grow. I've watched Christ grow in every member of my family and make them more attractive and more lovable every day. I watched Him completely turn my brother around as He has done for so many others.

My brother was an undercover agent (a "narc"). He worked heroin traffic in the streets and in the ghetto. He was mean, tough, bitter, rebellious. The church was not his favorite hangout.

I watched that man weep as Christ moved into his life and gave him peace.

I'm convinced Christ can do it for you, too. It happens in the quietness of your heart as you open the door to your life and by faith receive Him.

Those of us in youth work have always been aware that the odds of a person's becoming a Christian after age 18 are only about 15 percent. That is, around 85 percent of those who reject the opportunity during their teenage years will never see heaven.

If you feel a need to receive Him into your life, just close your eyes, lay your head back, and pray the most sincere prayer of your life. The moment you ask Him in, He is there forever. Thank Him for a new beginning. Thank Him for eternal, abundant life!

Get Growing

When you become a Christian, life has started all over again. Jesus told a "big brass" religious leader in John 3 that he had to be born again to get to heaven. When you give your life completely to Jesus, you're a brand-new person.

Too many Christians, however, continue to practice the same old sins. Jesus said, "If you love Me, you will keep My commandments" (John 14:15). First John 1 says that if we say we love Jesus and continue to practice sinning, we're lying. Revelation 3:15 says to be totally sold out to Jesus (red hot). To be lukewarm in our commitment is worse than no commitment at all.

How do I keep from stumbling?
How do I wait for my wedding?
How do I get to heaven?
How do I become lovable?
How do I find happiness?
How do I become a good wife, husband, father, mother?
The answer to all the above is to receive Christ and then grow.

For a newborn baby to live, he eats, breathes, sleeps—grows! When a baby Christian starts life, he reads God's Word, prays, spends time with other Christians (yes, even on dates), and tells others of his relationship with Christ.

It doesn't come all at once any more than a baby runs a 100-yard dash in 10 seconds, but it begins, and it grows. My goal is to get a little more like Jesus every day so that when death comes, it will be "just one step closer."

Growing Christians get more attractive every day. The reason Debbie-Jo is more appealing to me every day (after almost 25 years of marriage and four children) is that each day as she grows in Christ, she becomes more like Him. She's more lovable because Christ is the most lovable person ever. Wow! I get excited thinking about how terrific that is! In a world where people "fall out of love" because they think their spouse is getting "old," my wife is getting prettier all the time.

I could give you many more good reasons to grow, but you also need to know that the Bible doesn't just encourage your growth; it commands it. I meet so many young Christians who "receive Christ" and expect to just coast into heaven and never have another problem. They have to fall on their faces before realizing they must grow.

Years ago, my dad and I planted a row of 200 pine trees in some heavy Bermuda grass. Many didn't get enough water to grow quickly above the grass. The Bermuda literally strangled the new trees to death. Only those that grew stronger and taller than the grass survived.

You've got to grow tall and strong in Christ to get above all the temptations that want to bind you and strip the best from your new life in Christ. It's a matter of survival!

Want to get started?

First, quit crawling and get on your feet! Watch out! You

might fall, but your legs will get stronger with every step. It's interesting that when our four toddlers started walking (finally), they never liked to crawl again. They didn't look back at the crawling stage; walking is so much better. Don't look back! Keep walking one step at a time. "One thing I do: forgetting what lies behind and reaching forward to what lies ahead, I press on toward the goal for the prize of the upward call of God in Christ Jesus" (Philippians 3:13-14).

Second, set your standards high! Your will is so important. Learn to say no to things that you know will make you fall. The Lord will give you the power to live out your convictions. Reach for the sky. Allow God to help you be the best Christian you can possibly be! Wake up in the morning and smile as you say, "Lord, be my strength today. Let me be Your suit of clothes. Live inside of me, and make today the best we've ever had together."

Third, confess your sins regularly. First John 1:9 says, "If we confess our sins, He is faithful and righteous to forgive us our sins and to cleanse us from all unrighteousness." Confessing means to do two things. One, you're saying, "Lord, that was wrong." To confess means to see the sin as God sees it and be willing to admit it was a mistake. Two, you're saying, "Lord, thank You for dying and paying for that sin."

Too often, we sin "retail" and confess "wholesale." We sin in our attitudes and actions a hundred times a day, it seems, and then at night we say, "Lord, forgive all those sins today." Confess each sin as it happens. If you're unsuccessful at giving that sin to God and turning completely from it—that's called repentance—please don't quit talking to God about it! Keep the telephone ringing! He knows it all anyway, but He can only help you as you talk to Him and allow Him to work with you!

Take God with you as you go, even if it's back into that

sinful situation. Often you'll be able to turn from the problem immediately. At times, however, you'll be one of us many strugglers who have to take God with us again and again before we can get freedom from a particular sin.

Fourth, get to know Jesus. He's your best friend!

- He is taking you to the Father in heaven (see John 14:6).
- He is giving you the power to live happily (see John 10:10).
- He is making you a real lover (see John 13:34-35).
- He is causing everything that happens to you to turn out for your good (see Romans 8:28).

How do you get to know a friend?

You talk to him and listen to him, right? Prayer is talking to Jesus, your indwelling Friend. It's a lot simpler than it's often made out to be, but man, is it effective! To think that God is in touch with you and that He cares what you want and need is amazing. It changes your life! Always pray to God "in Jesus' name." It's through Jesus that our requests are answered (see John 14:13-14). Talk to Him about everything. Tell Him how much you love Him and appreciate all He's done for you. Take your problems to Him and give them to Him!

The old Ford van couldn't go fast enough as we flew through the night on Interstate 70 across the seemingly never-ending state of Kansas. The road between Steamboat Springs, Colorado, and Branson, Missouri, was too long for the ever-increasing contractions of childbirth to tarry. My bride of two years to the day was giving birth to our first little girl, and I had been skiing many miles away with my Young Life youth-group kids. Debbie-Jo was three weeks premature with the unexpected labor.

I felt like the most helpless and neglectful husband on earth when I called to wish her a happy anniversary and heard her first sighs of labor. After I hung up the phone and gathered my high-school kids, we scurried to our rooms, stuffed our ski clothes in our bags, and packed the van as fast as we could. We drove through the night; the giant, orange ball of a December mid-night's full moon rose dead center on the highway before us.

I prayed for a safe delivery, knowing that at any minute, the little girl who would one day own my heart could end her eight months of secure growth in her mommy's womb. Then she would take her first breath of life as the daughter I'd prayed for and dreamed about since I fell in love with her mom more than three years before.

No New Year's Eve party will ever touch the feelings of euphoria I experienced that December 31 morning as I hus-tled wildly through the hospital to the bedside of my lifetime lover. She was resting peacefully and had mastered a difficult delivery like a champion. I grabbed my "daddy identification card" and made my way to the newborn nursery in a stupor of amazement. A girl, a baby girl. Good grief, I couldn't believe that I could be so blessed! I loved her mom so much that I always wanted to see through her offspring a glimpse of her childhood. Now my greatest longing had come true.

As I stood in front of the large window, waving my pink card to the nurses inside, my eyes raced across 15 or 20 pink and wrinkled, diaper-clad forms of life. Then in an instant, I captured a view I'll never forget of the most picture-perfect baby I've ever laid eyes on. (Yes, all dads feel that way when they see with love-blinded eyes.) I knew she had to be mine. The nurse finally saw my baby ID card and wheeled the little crib over to the window. I gazed at her tiny fingers and perfect little features. Feelings of pride and deep appreciation filled my heart in a way that I'd never felt before. Jamie was a nine-pound answer to a big, big prayer.

I've prayed for friends; I've prayed for wisdom. I've prayed for patience; I've prayed for pain. I've prayed specifically for countless blessings, and God (although not always on my timetable) has shown me over and over that He's very serious when He says, "Ask, and you will receive" (John 16:24).

But never has God answered a prayer with the magnitude of this one: "God, please give me a family to love." My first daughter, Jamie, was only the beginning of the finest answered prayer I've ever prayed.

Prayer is everything. I suppose I've prayed a million prayers. All answered. I really believe in God. He thinks enough of me and you to answer our call and do what is best.

The following is something you'll want to study tonight before you go to bed. It's a brief summary of the best, most interesting, and most helpful look at how to study the Bible that I've found. People always told me, "You need to study your Bible," and I got confused, frustrated, and guilty, because I'm no scholar and I didn't know how!

Dr. Howard Hendricks makes it so simple, however, and I've adapted his approach below. I'll always thank him for turning me on to "God's love letter to a kid like me."

Why Study the Bible?

1. *To keep you from sin.* Psalm 119:11 says, "Thy word I have treasured in my heart, that I may not sin against Thee." The Bible keeps you from sin. Someone once wrote in the inside cover of a man's Bible, "This Book will keep you from sin, or sin will keep you from this Book."

2. *To help you grow.* First Peter 2:2 says, "Like newborn babes, long for the pure milk of the word, that by it you may grow in respect to salvation." The Bible is the only way you can

grow up spiritually. How long have you been a Christian? How much have you grown? I was seven years old as a Christian (24 natural years old), and I was still "wearing diapers" and "waving a rattle" until Dr. Hendricks got me turned on to the Bible and I started growing up!

Like newborn babes, long for the milk! I'll never forget the night we brought Jamie home from the hospital. I was working long days at the time, and my few hours of rest at night were so important to me. I just knew Jamie would sleep all night. Hardly! Every three hours, Mount Saint Helens erupted in the baby bed! Talk about a scream! Debbie-Jo and I stumbled around the house trying to find the blooming bottle, warm it up (I scalded my arm testing the stuff), and plug it into her mouth! Instantly, a great calm would come over the house. That's the desire we need for the Word. As the baby grabs for the bottle, we need to grab for the Book. Get yourself a sturdy cover for your Bible, and carry it everywhere so that when you need to, you can take a few spiritual vitamins.

Howard Hendricks says, "Either you are in the Word and the Word is conforming you to the image of Jesus Christ, or you are in the world and the world is squeezing you into its mold."

How to Study the Bible

The Bible can be "read" in several different ways. You can scan it (read it casually); you can read it carefully; you can study it (taking notes and underlining thoughts); you can memorize it (verse by verse or even a chapter at a time); and you can meditate on it by thinking it over and over in your mind as you drive to school, go to sleep at night, wait for your date, and so on.

All of the above are good, and there's time for each of them. Scan it, read it, study it, memorize it, and meditate on it.

The most rewarding time for you will be your studying, memorizing, and meditating on God's Word. Here's some help:

1. *Read it like a love letter.* That's what it is! Have you ever had a girlfriend or boyfriend in another city? There's nothing (when you're "in love") like a love letter. I used to know exactly when the postman would hit our mailbox! I'd be counting the minutes and fly to the door when that little red, white, and blue car pulled into our driveway. If Debbie-Jo hadn't written, I'd be crushed. But when I got one, I'd be smilin' all afternoon. I'd read that "baby" over and over and over again! (And I liked 'em full of sweet words! It's kind of funny, looking back now at the things we said then! We thought we were the hottest thing in love poetry.)

Anyway, I love love letters. Debbie-Jo still writes me special notes now when I travel, and I still cherish every word!

The Bible is the greatest love letter ever written. God lowered Himself to the earth, lived love out for us to see, and went to the cross to say one thing: "I love you! You may be the worst thing on two feet, but I love you, and here's My letter to you to tell you each day how much I mean it."

2. *Read it as though it's literally the Word of God.* That's what it is! "All Scripture is inspired by God and is profitable for teaching, for reproof, for correction, for training in righteousness" (2 Timothy 3:16).

Realize, every time you pick up the Book, that you're picking up a miracle work! For centuries, the "scholars" have tried to prove it a myth, but the archaeologists are digging up new things every year that prove its accuracy! The prophecies (future predictions written thousands of years ago proving the Bible to be God's Word), like those of today's actions in the Middle East, are incredibly exact. One example (there are hundreds) is found in Revelation 9:15-16. The Bible said 2,000 years ago that in the final battle called Armageddon, an army of 200 million would come to fight in the Middle East (for the oil), and that army would come from the East (China). Nobody had even 200,000 soldiers then. But 2,000 years later, China boasted an army of (you guessed it) exactly 200 million.[1]

Three Important Steps When You Read

1. *Observation.* Look closely and see what the writer is saying in each verse. A good first exercise is to take Acts 1:8 and write down at least 25 things you see in that one verse. You may get excited and even go for 50.

2. *Interpretation.* What does it mean? Too much Bible study begins and ends here. Go heavy on steps 1 and 3. When trying to figure out meaning, be sure to take a verse in context. You've got to be careful not to "prove" something with just one verse. "In context" means how that verse compares and fits into God's whole Word. An example of taking a verse out of context is the way some engaged couples justify premarital sex by saying, "Well, I'm sure it's okay because the Bible says, 'Love covers a multitude of sins.'" According to God, it's certainly not okay, because in context, that verse doesn't even imply that premarital sex can be justified. You can really get yourself into trouble if you don't weigh the verse against God's whole Word.

3. *Application.* Most important, how does it apply to your life? How does this verse affect your dating life, your schoolwork, your family relationships, your friendships, your thoughts, and your actions at parties? Pray each time you read, "Lord, teach me something today, and let Your Word sink deeply into me so I can become more what You want me to

be." Then watch your life change! That's what happened to a 17-year-old boy who gave his life to Christ and wrote me recently:

Daniel

Right now, I'm so excited about life, I just can't show you on paper how I feel! If I were in your presence, I'd be jumping up and down! I'm growing a little each day as I read my Bible along with my <u>Handbook on Athletic Perfection.</u>

Seven Keys to Good Observation

1. *Read each verse imaginatively.* Use your mental creativity. When Paul was writing from the Roman jail, smell that dark, musty cell. When he was on the boat, traveling across the Mediterranean Sea, get in the boat and out on the deck. Feel the wind in your hair. Taste the salty spray as you breathe. When Jesus was teaching, get your sandals on and join the disciples. Paint the picture of each scene in your mind.

2. *Read it selectively.* Ask yourself and answer these questions of each chapter you study:

   A. *Who*—who are the personalities involved? Who's talking; who's listening? What is each person like?

   B. *What*—what's being communicated here? What is going on? Is it a miracle? Is it a great teaching?

   C. *When*—when in Christ's life or the life of the church is this taking place? Is it before or after the resurrection? Is it just before the cross? Imagine the intense drama of that day!

D. *Why*—why was this passage written? What's the significance of it?

E. *Where*—where is the setting, and how does that location compare to our own situation? Is it in Jerusalem (Washington, D.C.), Samaria (enemy territory), or the Sea of Galilee (Lake Michigan)?

F. *Wherefore*—so what? What does this mean to me? How does it apply to me? What should I do now or change about myself in response to this passage?

A great exercise here would be to study the episode in the Bible where Jesus calmed the storm in Mark 4:35-41. Apply (with pen in hand) each of the above questions to the passage.

3. *Read it prayerfully.* Pray before, during, and after each study time, "Lord, open my eyes, and speak to me through Your Word. Make me more like Your Son today."

4. *Read it thoughtfully.* Take your time, and really study it. The Bible doesn't give its juiciest fruit to the casual or lazy reader. Get into it!

5. *Read it possessively.* Own it! Memorize it! I can't tell you how exciting and rewarding it is to know various chapters by heart. You really begin to feel the action. It takes months for people like me to put a couple of chapters down to memory, but it is worth the time and effort!

6. *Read it reflectively.* Be like a cow chewing her cud. Think about it over and over in your quiet time.

7. *Read it repeatedly.* Every time you go back to a passage, you'll learn something new from it!

Two other steps of growth essential to your new life in Christ are spending time with other Christians and telling others about Jesus. This may seem funny to you, but you can find Christian friends in church, Sunday school, and youth groups. Sure, they're not perfect (neither are we), but you can make a contribution, and you need friends who are experiencing the same joy and struggles you are. Date Christians! Invite non-Christians to Young Life, F.C.A., Christian camps, Youth for Christ, church, and youth group. So many guys and girls fall in love with non-Christians, and the result is often disastrous. Talk about "in-law" problems! Your Father is God, and a non-Christian's is Satan; your goal is heaven, and his is self-satisfaction. All too often, while trying to win him to Christ, he chips away at your morals. You compromise, and down you go. Keep your standards high!

When you make a new friend, you like to introduce him around to your other friends. Get Jesus out of the backseat of your car and let Him ride right beside you everywhere you go!

If you meet a friend at the Dairy Queen who asks you, "How are you doing?" you can say, "Man, great—really great!"

"What's so great about today?"

He'll be shocked at your answer! "Sit down for a minute, and let me tell you about the greatest thing that ever happened to me." Then you'll tell him lovingly how you became a Christian and the change Christ has made in your life! It is so much fun . . . and talk about growing! Those are the high points of your spiritual growth chart! Share with your friend the chapter of this book entitled "The Perfect Guest," and pray that he or she will come alive to Jesus Christ.

I'll never forget the leap I took the day I shared my faith with a friend for the first time. Before I became a Christian, I had been running around with a guy who did some pretty crazy things. Christianity was the furthest thing from his mind! I was 17 when I went away to camp and learned how great the Lord is. I asked Jesus into my life. When He came in, my desires began to change. I knew my friend's desires would have to change, too, or we wouldn't be spending much time together anymore.

I was really scared about how he'd respond to the new me. Would he think I was weird? I began to pray that God would give me the strength to tell him what was going on inside me. The day after camp was out, I went straight to his house. I said, "Wes, something really neat has happened to me. I became a Christian this summer." Expecting to get laughed at or smashed in the face, I prepared myself.

Instead, he came back with words I'll long remember. He began to tell me about an experience he had had at the time I became a Christian. He said he was going into a mountain curve late one night at his normal speed (twice the speed limit), and he lost control of his car. Instead of going over the edge and killing himself, miraculously it seemed, his car was on the other side of the curve, going straight again. He felt that God was speaking to him and there was a purpose in his being saved. He was waiting for someone to tell him what was going on in his head! Did I have fun telling him! Whoopee! What an answered prayer! Every time I've shared my faith since, it has been a mountaintop experience for me. To feel God's power working inside of meager little me is just too much to handle!

I'm excited to grow as a Christian each day I live. I can't wait for tomorrow!

This chapter on growing as a Christian is only a fraction of a start to an endless adventure of progress in your faith. The good news is that along with the vast challenges confronting a Christian in our day is a library of resources surpassing the needs you'll experience.

There are cassette-tape libraries with every inspirational

speaker you can imagine speaking on every phase of the Christian life. There is always a Bible at your fingertips. There are Bible studies, prayer groups, dedicated youth leaders, and vibrant churches springing up everywhere. But you have to want it. You must be motivated to put Christ number one and to grow up in Him or it will never happen.

The exciting movie *The Wiz* was Motown's moving version of *The Wizard of Oz*. At the conclusion, as Dorothy (Diana Ross) stood before the great Wiz, tears rolled out of her beautiful, brown eyes when she sang and dreamed of going home! She wanted to go home, and she wanted it more than anything else in the world. The Wiz was telling her that if you want something bad enough, you'll find it. That's faith. That's growth. When you desire it so deeply that it moves you into action, you'll always find it, and love will be the result of your quest.

God gave me love at a time when I needed it the most. What a moment it was, almost 25 years ago, when Debbie-Jo walked down the aisle in her beautiful, white gown. How terrific it was to be able to look forward to a life of Christlike love with a girl I so admired and respected. With God in your life, it's still possible to wait for His timing with sex. The trust and love that we now share make every day we live sweeter than the day before.

With the love God can give you and the complete forgiveness that Jesus has made possible, you can expect the same!

The Constitution:

The Power of the Written Word

Fifty-five men in the Constitutional Convention (53 of them staunch evangelical Christians) clearly designed our nation as a king-sized bed for the prospering haven and growth of the multi-denominational Christian faith.

> You do well to wish to learn our arts and ways of life, and above all, the religion of Jesus Christ. These will make you a greater and happier people than you are. Congress will do everything they can to assist you in this wise intention.
> —GEORGE WASHINGTON[1]

> I now offer you the outline of the plan they have suggested. Let an association be formed to be denominated "The Christian Constitutional Society," its object to be first: The support of the Christian religion. Second: The support of the United States.
> —ALEXANDER HAMILTON[2]

> It cannot be emphasized too strongly or too often that this
> great nation was founded, not by religionists, but by Chris-
> tians; not on religions, but on the gospel of Jesus Christ!
>   —PATRICK HENRY[3]

Those well-intended Founding Fathers built a future for
manger scenes in every city park at Christmastime, crosses
atop every schoolhouse, and New Testaments on every schoolhouse desk. They specifically wrote God's Word onto the stone
walls of their government buildings, appointed Christian
chaplains to their army, read Scripture at every legislative ses-
sion, used Scripture as the benchmark of every Supreme Court
ruling, put a Bible in the saddlebag of every Pony Express rider,
and used Scripture in every school textbook on every subject
from biology to literature to law.

Those men had a written Constitution that in less than
200 years made America the most envied, most powerful, and
richest nation in the history of the world.

Today, the Constitution is being bent, fragmented, broken, and misinterpreted, and our nation is spinning in a whirl-
wind of crime and moral decline.

I am convinced that every man and woman who wants to
live at the top of the world in terms of a life of real love, real
inner peace, and real fulfillment needs a clear, written constitution describing the values he or she cherishes and the boundaries he or she will not forsake.

Do you have one yet?

When Satan sought to distract and dethrone Jesus in the
wilderness that fateful day near Jericho, each time Satan threw
out the bait on the trap, Jesus responded as resolutely as an
eagle soars above the treetops, "It is written." "It is written." "It
is written."

He had a personal constitution, and He knew it by heart. I've been working on mine for 20 years. I wish I would have written one at age 13! I've refined it; clarified it; looked for loopholes and trimmed them away; and used it more times than I can remember. Without it, I'm sure I'd be flat on my face today. I'm an expert at rationalization when I want something, but my personal constitution holds me to the line I want to live by.

As a man, as a husband, as a dad, and as a professional, I need to have my boundaries as clearly defined as a graduating high-school senior on the night of the prom.

If you want to insure a productive life with no regrets, dive into this chapter with both feet the way a red-tailed hawk swoops emphatically upon his prey with talons extended.

You can assure yourself that your deep valleys of failure will be minimized and your snow-capped peaks of triumph will be maximized. Here are some guidelines:

1. Make your perimeters crystal clear. The allurement of desire creates masters of deception. The eyes of lust propagate geniuses of rationalization. For example, for me and my staff, we know that our self-control is so weak that we've elected not to drink even one drop of alcohol. Although it has been a major stumbling block for many of us before, since that statement went into our constitution 25 years ago, even the desire has been a big fat zero.

2. Make it specific. Use measurable goals. If our U.S. Constitution's writers would have been a little more specific on their desires for religious freedom and the sanctity of life, the godless Supreme Court rulings that allow millions of murders of unborn children and the banning of prayer, the Ten Commandments, and Bible usage in schools would have never happened.

When the movie rating system first came out 20 or so years ago, my wife and I rented this PG-13 movie. It took the name of my Father in heaven in vain and belittled sex to the point of a joke. I added to my constitution that night that I'd never watch another movie. Don't you hate it when somebody cusses out your mom or your dad or makes fun of the girl or boy you love and how you love them? Man, that pushes my button. PG-13 means major sex language. R means extreme decadence. NC-17 and X are synonymous. (Sick.) Although magazines, records, and certain parties, dates, bands, and so on aren't rated, it doesn't take a rocket scientist to evaluate their intentions.

3. Make it bold. My mentor Howard Hendricks says, "Aim low and you'll get there every time." The marines get some of the finest when they say, "We're looking for a few good men." A tiny 10-year-old gymnast is a one-in-a-million athlete when she sticks a full-twisting layout back flip on the balance beam. She's filled with exhilaration, and the crowd comes to its feet in unison. But when a man and woman engage in sexual intercourse in the purity of their Hawaiian honeymoon, minds unhampered with pictures of "Miss October," thoughts unscathed by sadomasochistic and Led Zeppelin lyrics of "Do it till you're black and blue" pounded into their brains, hearts untarnished by high-school romances numbers one, two, three, four, five—that honeymoon, my friends, dwarfs any Olympic gold medal like the shadow of a basketball over a tiny BB.

4. Tear out your constitution, and post it on your dresser mirror or in your billfold, where you can be reminded of it often.

5. Finally, rewrite it when you find a loophole or a soft spot. Remember, the higher you reach, the more fantastic the view.

Oh, yes, by the way, let me issue a warning so you won't be surprised when it happens. The critics will be numerous. They'll call you legalistic, fanatic, fundamentalistic, whateveristic. Let 'em jeer. You can laugh all the way to the Maui Hilton.

Personal Constitution
God's Blueprint

The Eyes: (Psalm 101:3)
"I will set no worthless thing before my eyes; I hate the work of those who fall away; it shall not fasten its grip on me."

The Ears: (2 Timothy 1:13)
"Retain the standard of sound words which you have heard from me, in the faith and love which are in Christ Jesus."

The Tongue: **taste:** (Proverbs 20:1)
"Wine is a mocker, strong drink a brawler, and whoever is intoxicated by it is not wise."
speech: (Colossians 4:6)
"Let your speech always be with grace, seasoned, as it were, with salt, so that you may know how you should respond to each person."

The Touch: (1 Corinthians 6:18)
"Flee immorality. Every other sin that a man commits is outside the body, but the immoral man sins against his own body."

The Mind: (Philippians 4:8)
"Finally, brethren, whatever is true, whatever is honorable, whatever is right, whatever is pure, whatever is lovely, whatever is of good repute, if there is any excellence and if anything worthy of praise, let your mind dwell on these things."

The Heart: (Psalm 119:11)
"Thy word I have treasured in my heart, that I may not sin against Thee."

Personal Constitution
My Standard

The Eyes: I will _____
_____
_____

The Ears: I will _____
_____
_____

The Tongue:
   taste: I will _____
_____
_____

   speech: I will _____
_____
_____

The Touch: I will _____
_____
_____

The Mind: I will _____
_____
_____

The Heart: I will _____
_____
_____

The Greatest Gift

John 3:16

"*For God*
(the greatest lover)
so loved
(the greatest love)
the world,
(the greatest need)
that He gave
(the greatest commitment)
His only begotten Son,
(the greatest life)
that whoever believes in Him
(the greatest offer)
should not perish,
(the greatest death)
but have eternal life."
(the greatest gift)

Appendix:
Creation vs. Evolution

A tremendous amount of fraud has been used to try to convince the general public that we live in a godless universe. Human beings have such a strong desire to "be their own bosses" and to get God out of their world that they have stretched the truth to the breaking point, attempting to advance Darwin's theory. Yet according to Genesis 1, we were divinely created in the image of God.

Nobel Prize winner and renowned physicist Dr. Arthur Compton said, "For myself, faith begins with a realization that a supreme intelligence brought the universe into being and created man. It is not difficult for me to have this faith, for it is incontrovertible that there was a plan, there is intelligence—an orderly, unfolding universe testifies to the truth of the most majestic statement ever uttered—'in the beginning, God.'"

Dr. Robert Jastrow, the astute Director of the Goddard Institute (NASA), agreed, "Now we see how the astronomical evidence leads to a Biblical view of the origin of the world. . . . The astronomers are so embarrassed by this that for the scientist who has lived by faith in the power of reason, the story ends like a bad dream. He has scaled the mountain of ignorance, he is about to conquer the highest peak when he finds himself face-to-face with a group of theologians who have been there for centuries!"[1]

The world's foremost paleontologist (and not a creationist himself), Dr. Colin Patterson, the Chief Paleontologist for the British Museum of Natural History, candidly rebuffs his own opposing view of God's divine act of creation when he says, "How can I study evolution for 15 years and learn nothing from it? Evolution not only conveys no knowledge, it seems to convey 'anti-knowledge.'"[2]

Nobel Prize winning physicist from Harvard Dr. George Wald joined Dr. Patterson in a confession of honesty tragically rare in the pseudo-scientific field of evolution: "There are only two possible explanations as to how life arose. Either spontaneous generation leading to evolution or a supernatural creative act of God. Spontaneous generation leading to evolution was scientifically disproved 120 years ago by Louis Pasteur and others. But that leaves us with only one other possibility, that life arose as a supernatural act of God. I don't want to believe in God, therefore I choose to believe in that which is scientifically impossible, spontaneous generation leading to evolution."[3]

Darwin himself confesses in his own book *Origin of the Species* that fueled the original fire of the humanistic quest for meaning of life without God: "To suppose that the eye, with all of its inimitable contrivances for adjusting the focus to different distance, for admitting different amounts of light, and for the correction of spherical and chromatic aberration, could have been formed by natural selection, seems, I freely confess, absurd in the highest degree."[4]

The pillars of Darwin's theory are the pillars of Darwin's downfall. My book *Darwin's Demise* published by Master Books details the sheer impossibility of spontaneous generation and species evolution.

Jesus, the only God-man and who was actually there with God at creation, did not mince words when He said: "But from the beginning of creation, God made them [Adam and Eve] male and female" (Mark 10:6).

Darwinian Evolution: A Faulty Foundation

An agnostically driven scientific world enthusiastically boarded Charles Darwin's revolutionary ship in 1859 leaving God out of the creative process. Before half a century had passed, the majority of the "intellectual elite" (with agnostic or atheistic bias) had applied their spiritual blinders and turned his ill-founded theory into "scientific-fact." During the ensuing 20th century, most high-school and college biology textbooks presented Darwin dogma, disregarding the overwhelming scientific evidence toward the contrary.

The four foundational pillars of Darwin's theory are (1) good mutations, (2) spontaneous generation, (3) natural selection, and (4) survival of the fittest. Without a degree in any field of science and a blatant bias against his father's faith (Darwin once said "The Old Testament was no more to be trusted than the beliefs of any barbarian. . . . I can hardly see how anyone ought to wish Christianity to be true."), Darwin postulated ideas that stretched the human imagination. As Dr. D. V. Ager, President of the British Geological Association, concludes, "It must be significant that nearly all the evolutionary stories I learned as a student . . . have now been debunked."[5]

After 30 years of inquisitive study and extensive writing and lecturing on this fascinating subject, briefly (and I mean, briefly) I'd like to present the case for Darwin's demise and the Genesis resurrection.

Good Mutations: "No matter how numerous mutations may be they do not produce any kind of evolution."[6]—Dr. Pierre-Paul Grosse, former President of the French Academie des Science.

"Good mutations are so rare that we can consider them all bad."[7]—Dr. H. J. Muller

"The mass evidence shows that all, or almost all, known mutations are unmistakably pathological."[8]—Dr. C. P. Martin

Spontaneous Generation: From a lifeless ocean, Darwin and other scientists postulate that life spontaneously generated from a pool of lifeless matter.

"No geological evidence indicates an organic soup ever existed on this planet. Therefore, we may with fairness call this the myth of the pre-biotic soup."[9]—Dr. Charles Thaxton (Harvard), Dr. Walter Bradley (University of Texas), and Dr. Roger Olsen (Colorado School of Mines).

"The scientific probability that the simplest form of life spontaneously generated from non-life is 1 to $10^{2,000,000,000}$."— Dr. Carl Sagan. Professor Harold Morowitz states it as 1 to $10^{340,000,000}$.

NOTE: Dr. Emil Borel, who discovered the Law of Probability, frankly states, "The occurrence of any event where the chances are beyond one in one followed by 50 zeros is an event which we can state with certainty will never happen, no matter how much time is allotted and no matter how many conceivable opportunities could exist for the event to take place."[10]

Natural Selection: Darwin conceded that if his theory was true the number of intermediate transitional links between species must be "inconceivably great" in the fossil record.

Dr. Colin Patterson, regarded as the number one fossil scientist in the world, states, "There is not one such fossil [transitional form] for which we can make a watertight argument. . . . No one has ever created a species from natural selection, or even gotten near it."[11]

"All paleontologists know the fossil record contains precious little in the way of intermediate forms."[12]—Dr. Stephen J. Gould (Harvard)

Without good mutations, spontaneous generation, and natural selection there can be no transition between species, and survival of the fittest becomes a moot argument.

Darwin's Demise

"I believe one day the Darwinian myth will be ranked the greatest deceit in the history of science. When this happens, many people will pose the question, 'How did this ever happen?' "[13]—Dr. S. Lovtrup

Since the creation of the world God's invisible qualities—his eternal power and divine nature—have been clearly seen, being understood from what has been made, so that men are without excuse. For although they knew God, they neither glorified him as God nor gave thanks to him, but their thinking became futile and their foolish hearts were darkened. Although they claimed to be wise, they became fools. Romans 1:20-22, NIV

Every painting has a painter.
Every watch has a watchmaker.
Every book has a writer.
Every design has a designer.
Every computer has a programmer.
And every creation has a creator.

Notes

Chapter 5

1. *Teens & Aids—Playing It Safe,* 1987, American Council of Life Insurance and Health Insurance Association of America.

Chapter 7

1. Stan E. Weid, Ph.D., *Predicting and Changing Teen Sexual Activity Rates* (Salt Lake City, Utah: Institute for Research and Evaluation, July 1992), p. 28.

Chapter 8

1. Stan E. Weid, Ph.D., *Predicting and Changing Teen Sexual Activity Rates* (Salt Lake City, Utah: Institute for Research and Evaluation, July 1992), p. 28. Statistical charts for Illinois Adolescent Pregnancy Programs (figure 1).
2. *CQ Researcher,* published by Congressional Quarterly, Inc., 11/4/94, vol. 4, no. 41, p. 957.
3. Ibid.
4. *Weekly Reader* survey cited by Gannett News Service, November 1995; a recent survey by the National Institute on Drug Abuse, cited in *The Church Around the World,* October 1995.
5. Robert H. Stein, "Wine Drinking in New Testament Times," *Christianity Today,* 6/20/75, p. 10.
6. Homer, *The Odyssey,* 2 vols. (Cambridge, Mass.: Harvard University Press, n.d.), vol. 1, book IX, pp. 208f.

Chapter 9

1. MTV's *Week in Rock,* 5/12/95.
2. *Circus,* 10/10/78, p. 26.
3. *Broadcasting Magazine,* 2/15/88.
4. Song, "Sex. Murder. Art." (*Divine Intervention*), 1994.

5. Song, "Closer" (*The Downward Spiral*), 1994.
6. *Farm Journal,* 10/95.
7. Roper Youth Report, as reported in *Teachers in Focus,* 10/95.
8. Concert in Winterthur, Switzerland, *Kerrang!,* 9/30/95.
9. MTV's *Week in Rock,* 9/15/95.
10. *Kerrang!,* 10/7/95.
11. MTV's *Week in Rock,* 9/22/95.
12. From the *Lies* album, 1988.

Chapter 10

1. "Voices from High School: Maybe Parents Really Don't Under-stand," *The Dallas Morning News,* 3/8/92, p. 6F.
2. Gregory B. Davis and L. W. Schroeder, "Influence of Contact Angles on the Leakage of Latex Condoms," *Journal of Testing and Evaluation,* 9/90, pp. 356-57.
3. Robert Knight, "Fact Sheet on Condom Effectiveness," The Her-itage Foundation, Washington, D.C., 11/11/91.
4. William B. Versey, "Condom Failure," *HLI Reports,* vol. 9, no. 7, 7/91, pp. 1-4.
5. James Trussell, David Lee Warner, and Robert A. Hatcher, "Con-dom Slippage and Breakage Rates," *Family Planning Perspectives,* 1-2/92, pp. 20-23.
6. D. C. Strasburger, "Sex, Drugs, Rock 'n Roll: An Introduction," *Pediatrics,* 76:76:659, 1985.
7. *U.S. News & World Report,* 7/17/89.
8. Patricia Hersch, "Sexually Transmitted Diseases Are Ravaging Our Children: Teen Epidemic," *American Health,* May 1991, p. 44.
9. Family Research Council, *Free to Be Family,* 1992, pp. 28-29.
10. *Historical Statistics of the United States,* 93d Cong., 1st sess., House Doc. 93-78 (Part 2), p. 1140; U.S. Department of Commerce and U.S. Bureau of the Census statistics; John Keegan and Richard Holmes, *Soldiers* (New York: Viking, 1986), p. 154.
11. "Life Before Birth," *Life,* 4/30/65, reprint p. 9.
12. *Branson Daily News,* 12/95, p. 1.

13. M. Bulfin, M.D., "A New Problem in Adolescent Gynecology," *Southern Medical Journal,* vol. 72, no. 8, 8/79.

14. Margaret Carlson, "Abortion's Hardest Cases," *Time,* 7/9/90, p. 26.

15. Jessica Shaver, "Abortion Survivor," *Focus on the Family,* 3/95, p. 2.

16. "Study on Homosexuals Released," *AFA Journal,* 2/90, p. 3.

17. "Homosexuality According to Science." *Christianity Today,* 8/18/89, p. 27.

18. "Study on Homosexuals Released," *AFA Journal,* 2/90, p. 3.

19. Robert Steinbrook, "AIDS Costs Will Nearly Double by 1994," *Los Angeles Times,* 6/20/91, p. A6.

20. Theresa L. Crenshaw, M.D., "Ten AIDS Myths Answered," *AIDS Protection,* 9/89, p. 3.

21. Ibid.

Chapter 11

1. Josh Zweiback, "S.C.A.M.," *Westside Glance,* (1986), vol. 31, no. 5, p. 3.

2. William J. Bennett, *The Book of Virtues* (New York: Simon & Schuster, 1993), p. 475.

Chapter 13

1. *Time,* 5/21/65.

Chapter 14

1. George Washington, 5/12/1779, from his "Address to Delaware Indian Chiefs," in John C. Fitzpatrick, ed., *The Writings of George Washington from the Original Manuscript Sources: 1749-1799* (Washington, D.C.: Bureau of National Literature and Art, 1907), p. 1:64.

2. Alexander Hamilton, 4/16-21/1802, in writing to James Bayard, in Allan M. Hamilton, *The Intimate Life of Alexander Hamilton* (Philadelphia: Richard West, 1979), p. 335.

3. Quoted in David Barton, *The Myth of Separation* (Aledo, Tex.: WallBuilder Press, 1991), p. 118.

Appendix
1. Dr. Robert Jastrow, *God and the Astronomer* (W.W. Norton, 1978).
2. Dr. Colin Patterson, Senior Paleontologist, British Museum of Natural History, London, in an interview on British Broadcasting Corporation (BBC) television, March 4, 1982. Patterson is a leading exponent of the new science of cladistics.
3. George Wald, late professor of Biology, Harvard University, "The Origin of Life," *Scientific American*, vol. 191(2) (August 1954), p. 46.
4. Charles Darwin, *The Origin of the Species*, (London: J.M. Dent & Sons, Ltd., 1971), p. 16.
5. "The Nature of the Fossil Record," in *Proceedings of the Geological Association*, vol. 87, no. 2, 1976, pp. 132-33.
6. *Evolution of Living Organisms* (New York: Academic Press, 1977), pp. 88-103.
7. "How Radiation Changes the Genetic Constitution," *Bulletin of the Atomic Scientists*, vol. 11, no. 9 (November 1955), p. 331.
8. "A Non-Genetic Look at Evolution," *American Scientists*, vol. 41, no. 1 (January 1953), pp. 100, 103.
9. Paul S. Taylor, *Origins Answer Book* (Mesa, Ariz.: Eden Productions, 1990), p. 76.
10. *Possibilities of Life* (Dover, NY: 1981).
11. *The Bible-Science Newsletter* (August 1981).
12. "The Return of Hopeful Monsters," *Natural History,* vol. 86 (1977), p. 22.
13. *Darwinism: The Refutation of a Myth* (London: Croom Helmm, 1987), p. 422.

FOCUS ON THE FAMILY®

teen outreach

At Focus on the Family, we work to help you really get to know Jesus and equip you to change your world for Him.

We realize the struggles you face are different from your parents' or your little brother's, so we've developed a lot of resources specifically to help you live boldly for Christ, no matter what's happening in your life.

Breakaway®
Teen guys
breakawaymag.com

Besides teen events and a live call-in show, we have Web sites, magazines, booklets, devotionals and novels ... all dealing with the stuff you care about. For a detailed listing of the latest resources, log on to our Web site at **go.family.org/teens**.

Focus on the Family Magazines

We know you want to stay up-to-date on the latest in your world — but it's hard to find information on relationships, entertainment, trends and teen issues that doesn't drag you down. It's even harder to find magazines that deliver what you want and need from a Christ-honoring perspective.

Brio®
Teen girls 13 to 15
briomag.com

That's why we created *Breakaway* (for teen guys), *Brio* (for teen girls 12 to 16), *Brio & Beyond* (for girls ages 16 and up). So, don't be left out — sign up today!

Brio & Beyond®
Teen girls 16 to 19
briomag.com

Phone toll free: (800) A-FAMILY (232-6459)
In Canada, call toll free: (800) 661-9800

BP06XTN

Want More? Life

Go from ordinary to extraordinary! *Want More? Life* will help you open the door to God's abundant life. You'll go deeper, wider and higher in your walk with God in the midst of everyday challenges like self-image, guys, friendships and big decisions. Spiral hardcover.

Want More? Love

You may ask, "Does God really love me? How can He love me — with all my faults and flaws?" *Want More? Love* is a powerful devotional that shows you how passionately and protectively God loves and cares for you — and how you can love Him in return! Spiral hardcover.